Dogs

BY
WILLIAM MOORES
AND
PADDY CUTTS

PRC

AUTHOR'S ACKNOWLEDGEMENTS

Due credit and thanks must go to Paddy Cutts for her patience and hard work in providing a representative selection of photographs in this book.

I would also like to record my grateful thanks to Janet Dodd, Alison Fletcher, Sara-Jane Green and Anne Williams for their help in the production of this book.

Thanks also to the many breeders and exhibitors who gave their time and made their dogs available for studio and location work.

All photographs are by Paddy Cutts/Animals Unlimited.

USEFUL ADDRESSES

UK

KENNEL CLUB
1-5, Clarges Street
Piccadilly
London. W1Y 8AB
Tel: 071 493 6651

OUR DOGS PUBLISHING CO. LTD.
5, Oxford Road Station Approach
Manchester
M60 1SX
Tel: 061 236 2660

DOG WORLD
9 Tufton Street
Ashford
Kent
TN23 1QN
Tel: 0233 621877

DOGS MONTHLY
RTC Associates
Ascot House
High Street
Ascot
Berks.
SL5 7JG
Tel: 0344 28269

DOGS TODAY
6 Station Parade
Sunningdale
Berks.
SL5 OEP
Tel: 0344 875442

EUROPE

FCI
Secretariat General
13 Albert
B653c Thuin, (Belguim)
Tel: 0233 621877

USA

AMERICAN KENNEL CLUB
51 Madison Avenue
New York
NY - 10010
Tel: 212 / 696 - 8200

DOG WORLD
Maclean Hunter Publishing
29 North Wacker Drive
Chicago
IL 60606 - 3298

DOG NEWS
Harris Publications
1115 Broadway
New York
NY - 10010

AUSTRALIA

AUSTRALIAN NATIONAL
KENNEL COUNCIL
P.O. Box 285,
Red Hill South,
Victoria 3937

NATIONAL DOG
Sterling Media Pty Ltd.
P.O. Box 670
Seven Hills
2147 NSW

SOUTH AFRICA

KENNEL UNION OF SOUTH AFRICA
6th Floor
Bree Castle
68 Bree Street
Cape Town, 8001
South Africa
Tel: 0027 / 021 2390

CONTENTS

INTRODUCTION

The dog has been man's guard, hunting companion and loyal
friend for thousands of years.

Fossils dating back 30 million years suggest a positive
connection to the carnivorous pack animal which roamed
the earth and the wolf-types from which specific breeds
have evolved.

It was as a loyal companion that man first realised the true
worth of the dog. Dogs with distinctive, unique qualities
were developed from the original flock guard and hunting
companion breed types. Man began to practise selective
breeding to produce specific types of dog, which possessed
the features and abilities required to undertake
certain activities.

Almost every country house painting collection in England
includes the white 'bichon-type' and tri-colour toy spaniel
much favoured in the sixteenth century courts of Europe and
offered as gifts to the ladies in court.

In Egypt the tombs of the Pharaohs featured paintings of
their most favoured hounds, and, as the Egyptians believed
that they were a prerequisite for the afterlife, models of the
hounds, often in solid gold, were buried with the Kings.
They were also represented on the tomb walls amongst the
hieroglyphics. Taking another step around the world the Far
East lays claim to the Pekingese, the temple dog of dynasties
past, which was also characterised frequently in Chinese art.

By the nineteenth century, many breeds had evolved and it
wasn't until 1873, when The Kennel Club was founded, that
any formal application of either sporting or non sporting
status was applied.

The British Empire extended far and wide overseas and many
unique breeds found their way back to Britain for the delight
and amusement of a Victorian society which was already
enthralled by that innovation, the zoo! Charles Cruft, Spratts
biscuit salesman extraordinaire, realised that there was
increased interest in and enthusiasm for dogs, and gave the
people the spectacle that they wanted. In 1886 he ran his first
Terrier show and developed this to become his 'Great show

of dogs and Exhibition of sporting appliances'. Cruft's name became synonymous with quality pedigree dogs and to this day this show, now a four day exhibition, attracts an annual entry of 20,000 dogs and huge media interest.

Breed classification is now split into six groups and for the purpose of this book we have adhered to these categories with a representation of breeds in the Hound, Gundog, Terrier, Utility, Working and Toy groups. The first three groups have seen few additions in the last 25 years, whilst the Working and Utility groups have been swelled by the inclusion of emergent European breeds, particularly those with strong 'pastoral' connections. In Europe some breeds are classified in different groups and in America, for instance, the Schnauzer is classified as a Terrier!

Personal preferences draw enthusiasts to different breeds. Media exposure can also give rise to a greater demand for a specific breed.

Portrayal of a cuddly puppy or an immaculately coated dog must be weighed against the simple fact that it may grow into a 30 kg (80 lb) adult dog with essential grooming and exercise demands of many hours per week. Dogs are entitled to be properly groomed and exercised. In a family this should be a shared responsibility.

Prospective owners should take the time to research and familiarise themselves with the needs of their favoured breeds. There is no better way than seeing and meeting the breeds themselves and discussing them with breeders and exhibitors, either at the larger championships or at the breed club shows.

The high quality photographs in this book present good examples of the breeds within each group. The development of each group is outlined and this is supplemented by a "Points to remember" section to help to remind the reader of the true nature and *raison d'etre* of the breeds in the group.

Dog ownership can be a great pleasure, but only as long as the high degree of responsibility involved is acknowledged. Prospective owners need to select their dogs with care, according to their circumstances, and, in particular, their time and space constraints.

If this book helps to make an informed choice and halts the impulsive buy or whim, then it has been worthwhile.

William Moores

HOUND GROUP

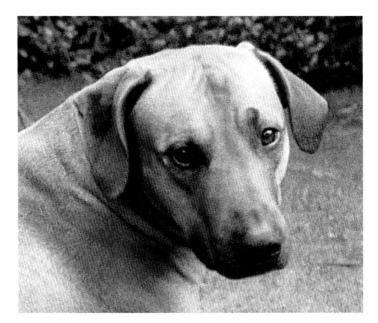

HOUND GROUP

The Hound group breeds can be broadly
divided into sight or scent hounds. The
traditional pack breeds, Beagles and
Bassets remain popular family pets, as
biddable and attractive as they are strong
willed on the scent.

Glamorous sight hound of the seventies
was the Afghan, a heavily coated breed
which requires a great deal of space
and exercise.

More suited to the modern pace of life,
the Dachshund in all six variations
remains popular, particularly the
Miniature Smooth and Miniature
Longhaired varieties.

Giant of the group is the Irish
Wolfhound, almost a metre high
(3.03 feet) at the shoulder but a breed
with a gentle, kind and friendly nature.
Still popular within the group is the
Rhodesian Ridgeback, originally bred to
assist Rhodesian game hunters in pursuit
of their quarry. They remain an
excellent, loyal dog and are protective of
their family.

A native of Scotland, the Deerhound
again has many loyal supporters and
remains a great favourite. Elegance,
dignity and humour are words which are
frequently used to describe this guardian
of the baronial fire place.

Regular sight hounds include the
Greyhound and Whippet each with its
committed devotees. The elegant Saluki
has a highly developed hunting instinct
and has been acclaimed as the fastest of
all dogs.

In recent years the group has been supplemented by the Petit and Grand Basset Griffon Vendéen from France, a rough coated 'basset' type, plus several examples of the Grand variety. Also from France is the similar red wheaten or fawn Basset Fauve de Bretagne.

Sporting breed owners must appreciate the instincts of these majestic dogs.

POINTS TO REMEMBER

All hounds, whether sight or scent,
are traditional sporting breeds and
so have a strong instinct to pursue.
This is sometimes wrongly
interpreted as single-mindedness
or mischievousness.

Consideration should be given to
the size and strength of these dogs.
The six varieties of Dachshunds
represent the smallest breeds in the
group. At the other end of the scale
Afghans, Greyhounds, Irish
Wolfhounds and Salukis represent
the larger varieties which naturally
demand more exercise, open spaces
and more time.

Hounds are majestic dogs and will
repay good care with devotion to
the family which is privileged to
own them!

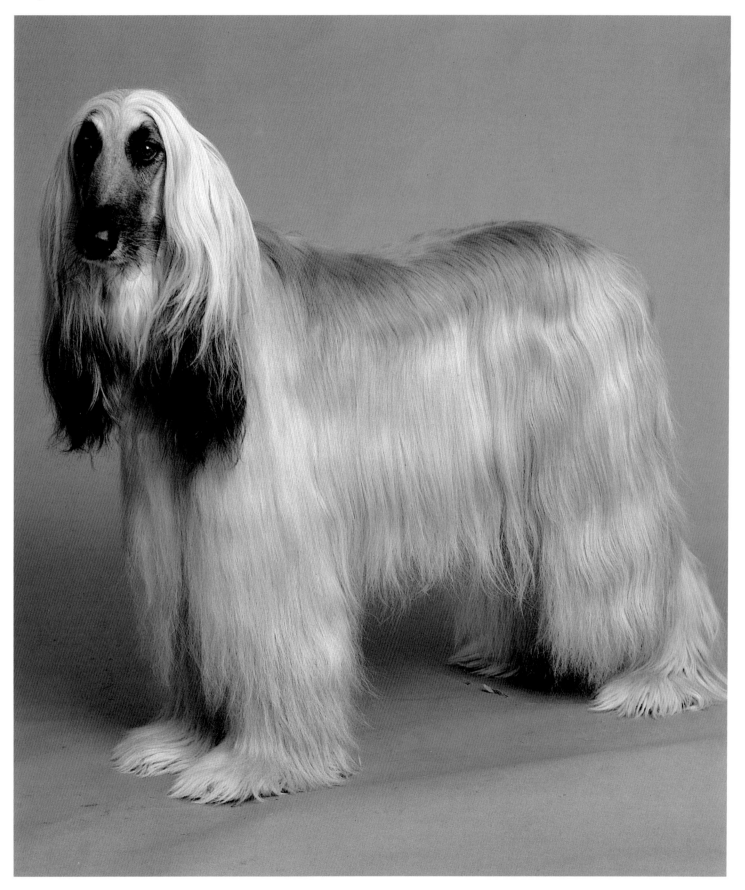

The elegant, aloof Afghan Hound.
Don't be deceived by that profuse
coat, beneath it is a strong and
agile sight hound.

Below: Afghan Hound puppies look most appealing in their 'woolly clip' - the makings of the Afghan's fine texture coat.

Right and overleaf: The Basenji (or barkless dog) is renowned for his chortle or yodel and his alert quizzical expression.

The Basenji was also said to have been a palace dog to the Pharaohs of ancient Egypt.

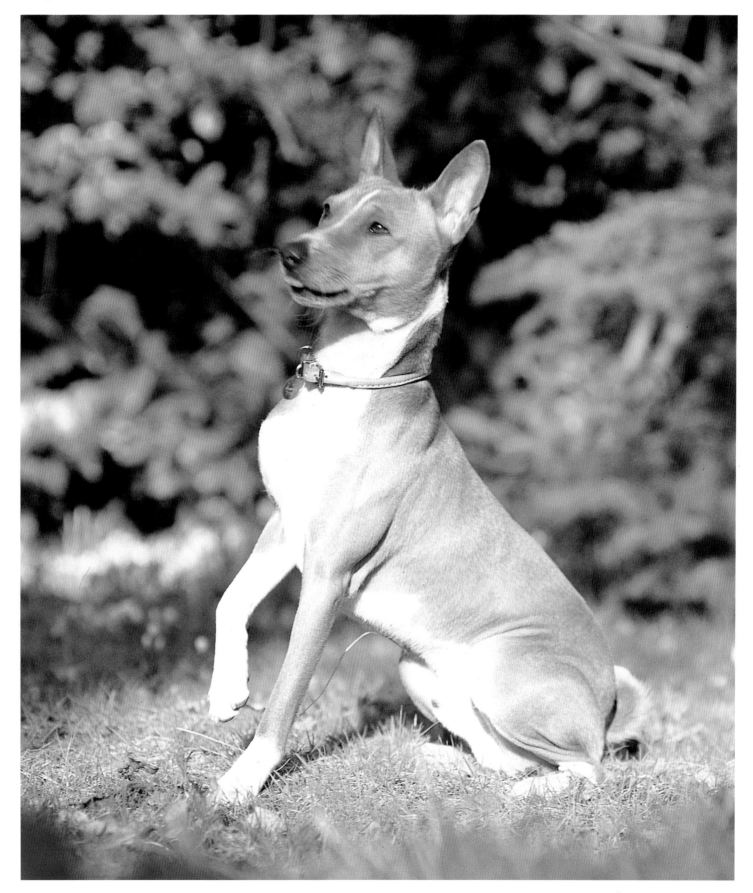

Right: The doleful expression of the long, low Basset Hound breed has great appeal. However, it is a strong, single minded scent hound.

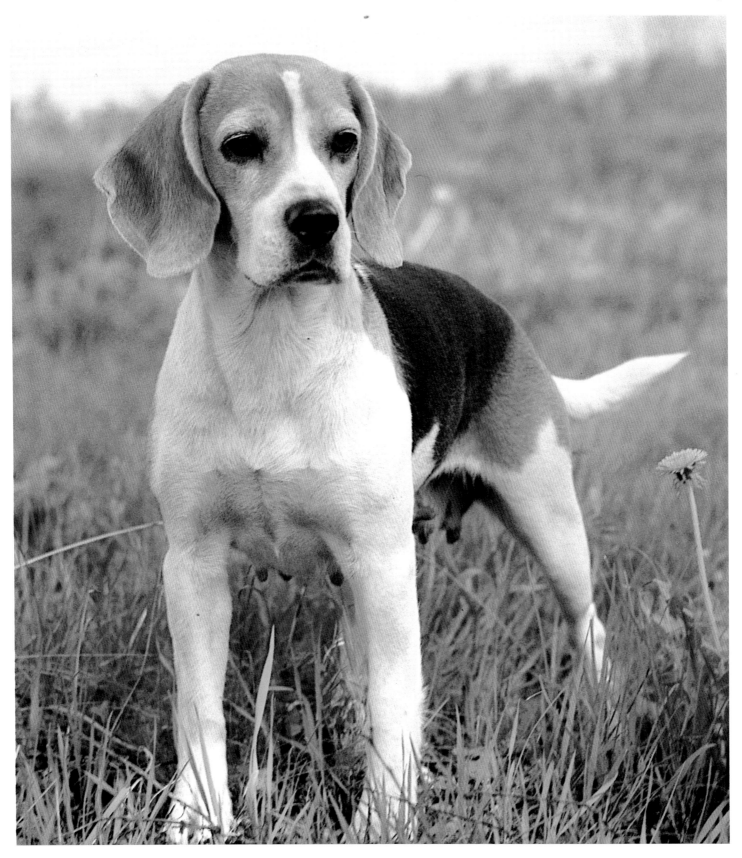

One of the oldest purebred British
hounds, the Beagle has become a
popular companion in the last 25
years. Its compact appearance and
smooth coat make it an
attractive hound.

Dogs

The Borzoi is an old established Russian hunting breed much favoured by the Czars. In 1892 HRH the Grand Duke Nicholas and Prince Oldenbourg entered a team of hounds at Crufts show. On numerous occasions over the course of the next few years the British royal family received these elegant hounds as gifts from their Russian counterparts. A natural sight hound, the Borzoi has a gentle nature, a muscular build and a tremendous turn of speed.

Dogs

The Miniature Long-haired Dachshunds pictured here show the unusual chocolate dapple (inset) and the attractive pale cream colours of coat. Essentially a hunting dog, they still possess a strong urge to pursue quarry 'to ground'.

This page: The Miniature Wire-haired Dachshunds here show their appealing 'beards' which add character to their expression. The Standard variety of Wirehaired is said to have developed as a result of cross-breeding between the Miniature Schnauzer and the Dandie Dinmont Terrier.

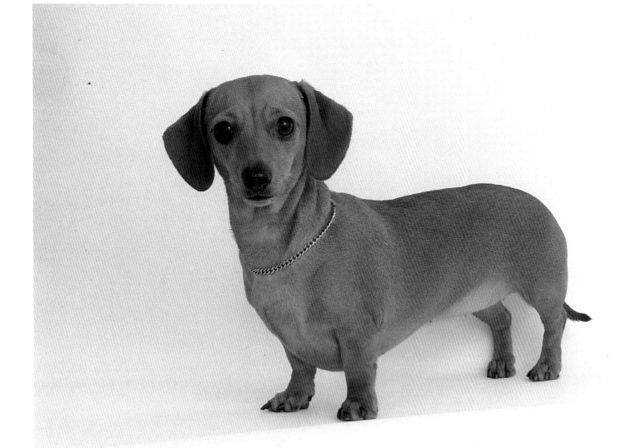

This page: Miniature Smooth-haired Dachshunds showing the popular tan coat (above) and the traditional black and tan variety. Their smooth coats require little grooming. **Overleaf:** Eyes left! Typical, quizzical expressions captured by the camera.

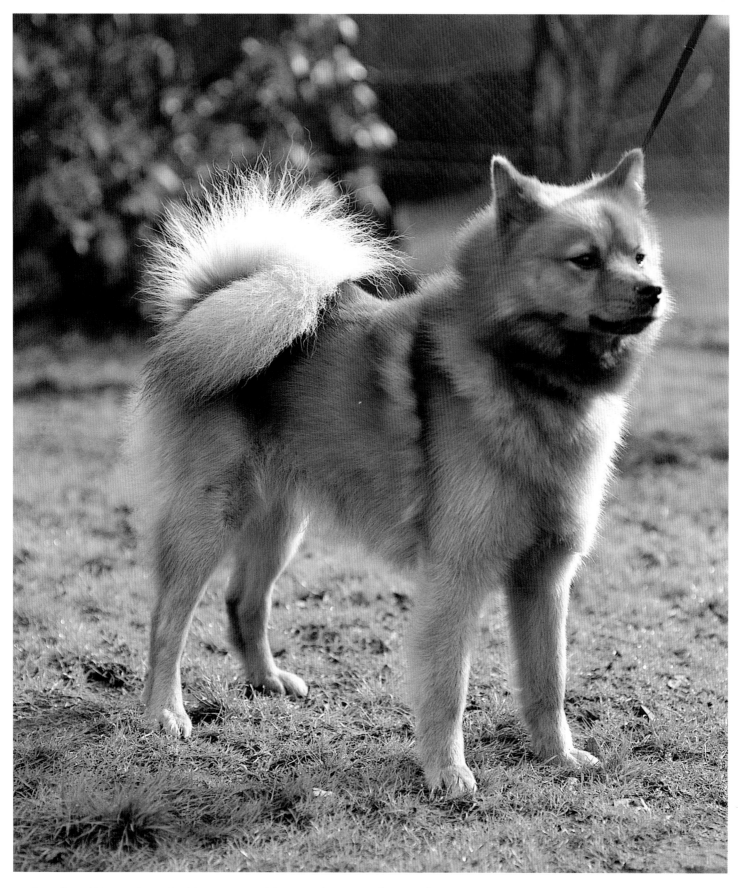

Left: The Elkhound is a bold spitz breed, capable of running his quarry for Scandinavian hunters. His dense, soft, woolly undercoat is complemented by a coarse, straight outercoat for warmth and weather resistance in colder climes.

Above: The Finnish Spitz has a distinctive mid length, red-gold or bright reddish brown coat. Its eagerness to hunt is obvious in its alert expression.

Dogs

In this litter of Finnish Spitz puppies it is easy to see the alert expression and the small, cocked, mobile ears.

Above: The Hamiltonstövare, or
Swedish Foxhound, is named after
Count Hamilton, the founder of
the Swedish Kennel Klub. It is a
well proportioned, stylish dog with
striking bold tri-colour marking.

Above: The Greyhound is a strong, muscular sight hound, probably the most familiar in this group. A dog of remarkable stamina, it is even-tempered and gentle. The racing 'cousin' to the show dog is out of a slightly smaller mould.

The Irish Wolfhound is the giant of all dogs, with the male standing 81-86 cm (32-34 inches) at the shoulder, and weighing at least 54.5 kgs (109 lbs). Despite their size they have a gentle nature with a soft expression which combines pride with calm.

The Petit Basset Griffon Vendéen
is an appealing 'basset type' from
Western France. His happy,
extrovert character endears him
to all.

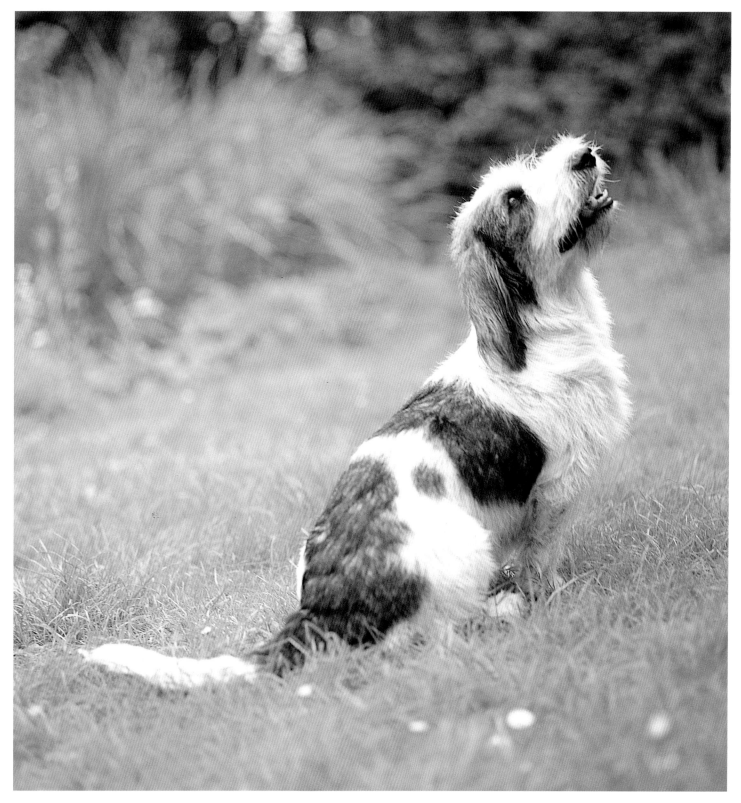

Above: The Grand variety of the Basset Griffon Vendéen type showing the typical harsh coat and alert expression.

Right: A native of Africa, where it assists big game hunters in running their quarry, the distinctive Rhodesian Ridgeback is a handsome, upstanding dog. The ridge of hair on its back grows in the opposite direction to the body coat.

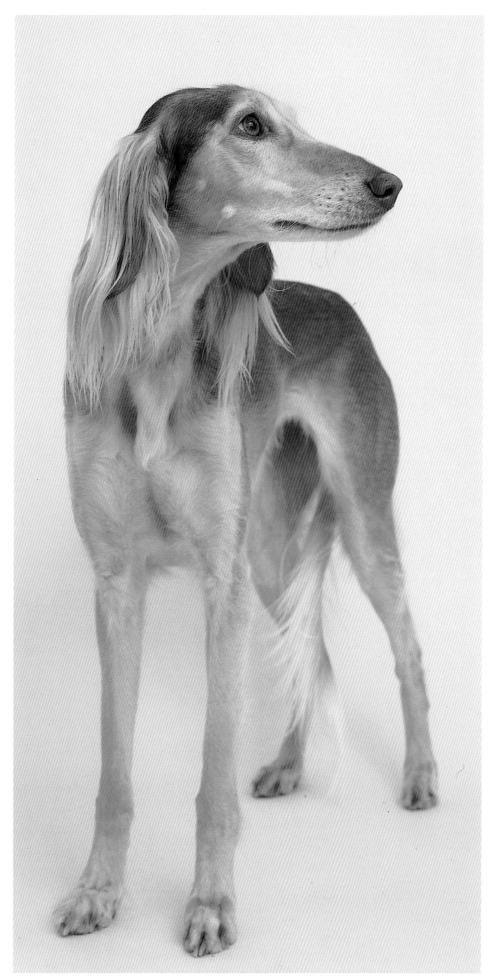

The elegant Saluki can be traced back in time to 329 BC, when it was known to be the domesticated companion to desert tribesmen. Another elegant sight hound, the beautiful ear featherings are displayed to advantage, and note those powerful hindquarters.

Overleaf: This lovely chocolate grizzle colour is sporting a traditional Arabian collar.

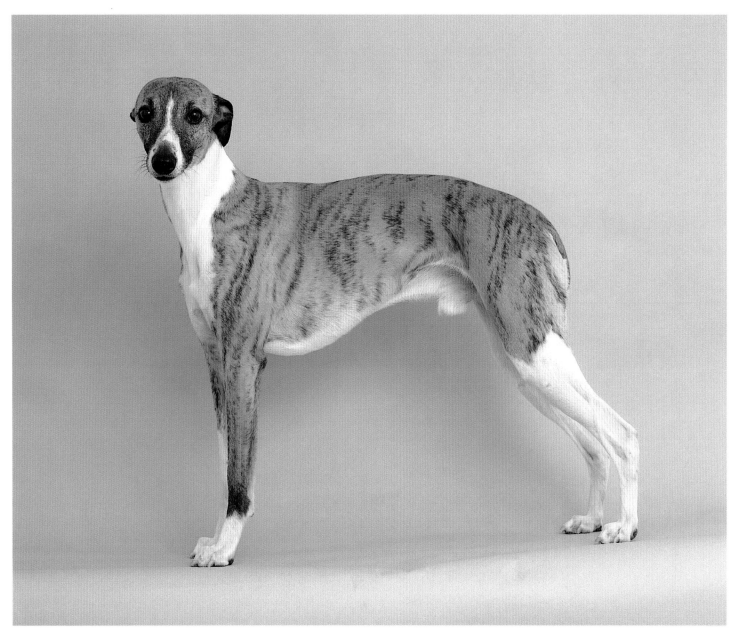

Above and overleaf: The Whippet is a small, muscular hound developed in England and almost certainly evolved from the Greyhound. Whilst Whippet racing was a popular pastime in late Victorian times, the Whippet Club was founded 100 years ago to promote the exhibition of the breed. Many colours and colour combinations are acceptable including this smart tan/brindle and white.

GUNDOG GROUP

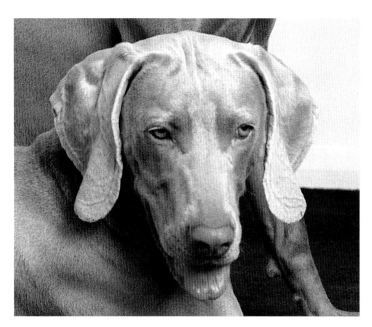

GUNDOG GROUP

The Gundog group includes the firm
favourite and currently the most popular
of all breeds, the Labrador Retriever.

This all round 'country gentleman' of
gundogs has maintained its place in the
top ten for many years. Its retrieving
ability and intelligence make it a
favourite with the shooting fraternity, as
a family pet or guide dog for the blind.

The Golden Retriever remains a firm
favourite along with the Cocker Spaniel
and the English Springer Spaniel.

These two Spaniels are also popular working dogs, although the divide between show and working strains is demonstrated by the smaller, lighter boned 'working cousins'. Nevertheless, their capability should not be underestimated.

'Minor' Spaniel breeds, the Sussex, Field, Clumber, Irish Water and Welsh Springer continue to attract interest, as do the emergent Hunt, Point and Retrieve (HPR) breeds from the continent.

The traditional Pointer, Gordon, English and Irish Setters have been joined by the German Shorthaired and Wirehaired Pointers, Hungarian Vizslas, Italian Spinoni and Weimaraners, which are sometimes described as the 'grey ghost' because of their striking colouration and piercing, light eyes.

The Setters have been re-joined in
recent years by the Irish Red and White,
a traditional breed out of the same stock
as the Irish Setter.

Gundogs need regular exercise and space
to run. Their intelligence and willingness
to please have to be acknowledged. These
sporting dogs usually attract active
owners who become committed
enthusiasts for life.

POINTS TO REMEMBER

All gundogs are highly intelligent
and eager to please.

Their basic instincts to retrieve or
'flush' game are evident in early
play and continue to develop. To
harness this natural ability
demands time and training in their
formative months. Consider this
when you fall for that adorable
bundle of fun.

Properly channelled, this
intelligence will produce a
sociable, well adjusted dog. Ignore
it, as people tend to do with
so many breeds, and it will
turn to boredom and
destructive tendencies.

Consider the size of the adult
dogs. For example, the popular
Labrador weighs in at 21-31 kilos
(60-70 lbs) and can attain half of
its adult weight at four months!

Described as the aristocrats of
dogs, gundogs deserve space, time
and training to realise their full
potential. Never underestimate
their intelligence.

Dogs

Right: The English Setter is one of the most glamorous of the Gundogs. His clean outline befits a stylish worker, cheerful companion and elegant mover. The stylish, tireless gait of all the Setters is one of their most attractive features.

Overleaf: An attractive tricolour (blue belton and tan) shown to advantage in a natural situation.

Right and overleaf: The intelligence of the German Shorthaired Pointer is captured in those attractive eyes.

One of the emergent HPR breeds from the Continent, the German Shorthaired Pointer was developed to satisfy the exacting needs of the sportsman and rough-shooter. The popular liver and white ticked colour is shown here.

Above: The German Wirehaired
Pointer is making its mark as a
medium-sized, all-purpose HPR
gundog. The breed is particularly
popular with rough shooters for its
performance in water and in the
field.

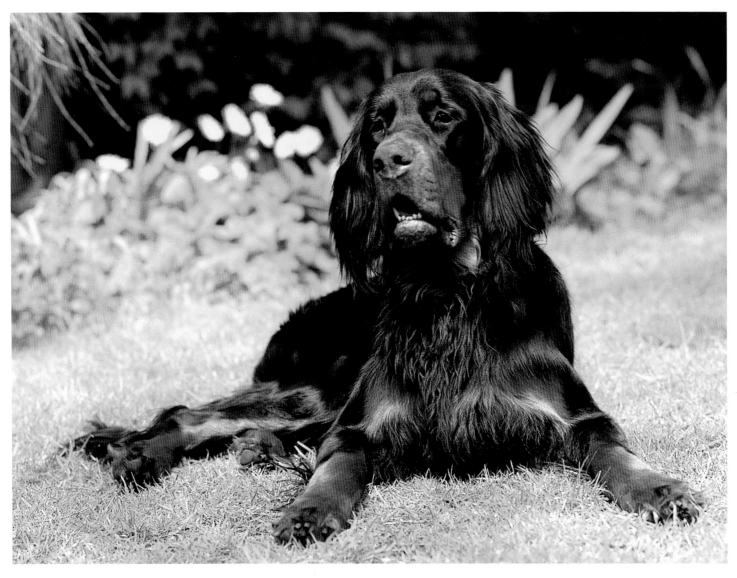

Above: The Gordon Setter has distinctive black and tan markings. The breed was developed on the estates of the Dukes of Gordon in Scotland.

Left: Another continental HPR breed is the Hungarian Vizsla, said to be a close cousin of the Weimaraner and German Shorthaired Pointer. The russet gold coat colour is unique to the breed.

Below and right: The Irish Setter has a magnificent rich chestnut coat and an attractive, elegant outline, making it the most popular of all the Setters. Its handsome, refined good looks belie a devilish sense of humour. Note the slightly greying muzzle of the older dog **(below)**.

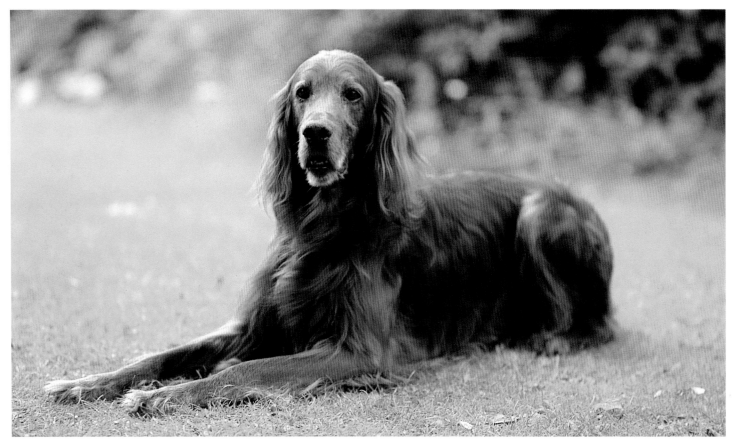

The Italian Spinone is thought to have originated in France, but gained popularity in northern Italy's Piedmont region as a sportsman's working companion. It is a big, squarely built dog with well muscled quarters. Here we see the attractive brown roan colouring and **overleaf** the striking orange.

Left: The Large Munsterlander is a medium-sized, multi-purpose continental Gundog, which has enjoyed rising popularity since it was first imported to the UK in the 1970s. Note the eager, alert expression.

Below: The Nova Scotia Duck Tolling Retriever originated from that Canadian province and is one of the smallest retriever breeds. Its thick coat insulates it well from the hostile conditions in which it is expected to work.

A Pointer quartering the ground on moorland eventually coming 'on point' to game is a magnificent sight. They instinctively track and indicate to air scent. The most popular colouring is liver and white, while black and white, orange and white or lemon and white is also acceptable.

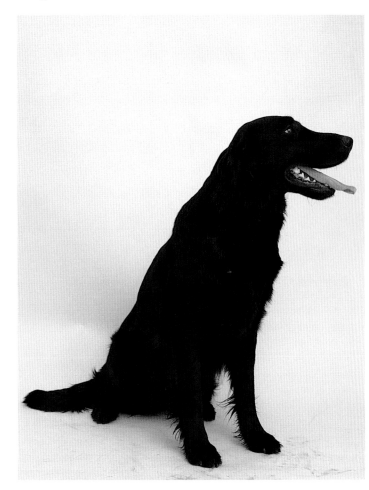

Above: The Flatcoated Retriever, or Wavy-coated Retriever as it was known, is an intelligent, medium-sized breed with a distinctive outline. The black **(left)** and liver **(right)** coats shown here are standard coat colours.

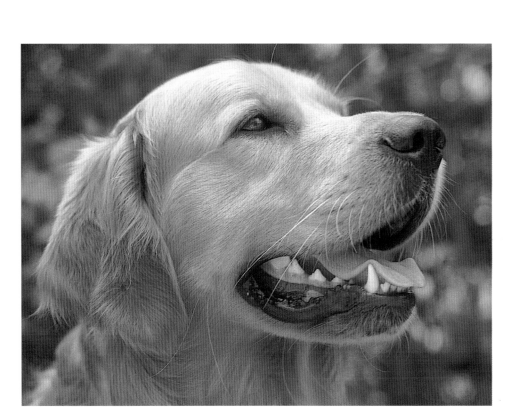

Right, opposite and overleaf: The Golden Retriever is another popular breed, whose happy disposition and melting smile have made it a favourite family pet. The 'bundle of fun' puppies become intelligent, confident dogs with natural working ability.

Above: The chocolate coloured Labrador Retriever is much sought after, being a rare coat colour compared to the popular black and yellow shown **overleaf**.

The loyal, biddable and intelligent Labrador Retriever is the most popular of all Gundogs. Beneath its dense outercoat lies a softer, weather resistant undercoat which protects it from extreme cold whilst swimming. The black is favoured by country sportsmen to the equally popular yellow seen in the show ring.

Above and left: The Clumber Spaniel was said to have been bred and developed by the Duke of Newcastle on the Clumber Park estate in Nottinghamshire out of stock imported from France over 200 years ago. This heavy boned Spaniel has its own Working Society dedicated to maintaining high standards in the field.

Right: The 'merry' Cocker is the most popular of all the Spaniel breeds. Always eager to please, its natural retrieving instincts are well known, as is the breed's 'flushing' ability. The breed boasts a range of coat colours, including solid (or self) colours. They enjoy plenty of exercise.

Opposite and left: The English Springer Spaniel is another cheerful extrovert. The oldest of sporting Gundogs, it was used to 'spring' game - hence the name. The breed is a popular family companion and the working strains produce many excellent dogs for the field.

Below and overleaf: Whilst the liver and white is more popular, the black and white is attractive and this one is complete with an undocked tail since the practice of tail docking for cosmetic reasons by persons other than vets was banned in the UK in 1993.

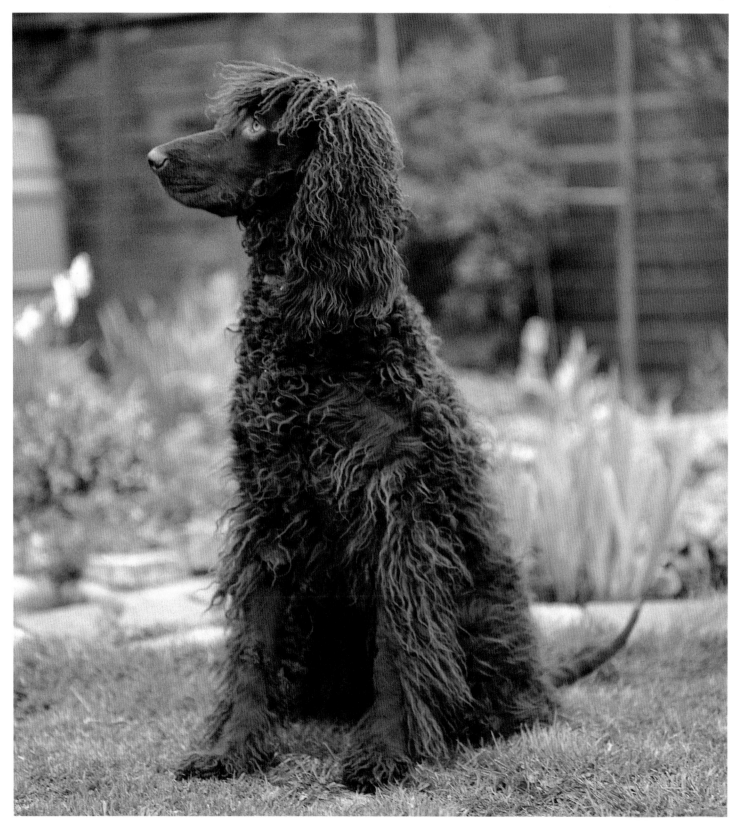

Above: A coat of tight ringlets makes the Irish Water Spaniel distinctive amongst the Spaniels. Dark liver in colour, the coat protects the tallest of the Spaniel family in the water. A versatile gundog, it is an excellent retriever and much favoured by wildfowlers.

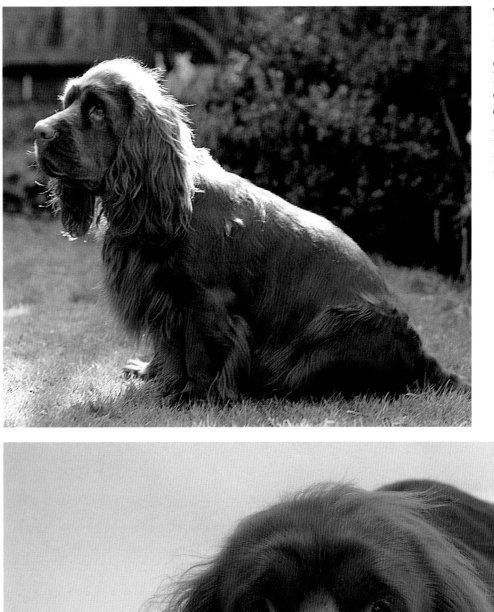

The Sussex Spaniel is one of Britain's traditional minor spaniel breeds originating from the county on the south coast which boasted huge sporting estates in the 18th century. The correct coat colour is described as 'rich golden liver'. Although not a speedy spaniel, its typical movement has a distinctive roll and its scenting ability equals that of other sporting spaniels.

The Weimaraner, or 'grey ghost', is another continental multi-purpose HPR breed specifically developed by the Dukes of the Weimar Republic to meet their exacting standards. Its striking colouration, light eyes and fearless but friendly temperament have endeared it to enthusiasts over the last 25 years.

TERRIER GROUP

TERRIER GROUP

The Terrier group's most popular breed is the West Highland White Terrier, a 'game' little dog with personality plus.

Like most of the terriers, his harsh coat requires regular care and attention. His close Highland associates, the Cairn, Scottish and Skye Terriers also remain firm favourites.

Completing the quintet from Scotland is the Dandie Dinmont, named after the much vaunted character in Sir Walter Scott's *Guy Mannering*. His soulful expression belies a workmanlike Terrier.

The Staffordshire Bull Terrier remains a firm favourite - witness the crowd several deep around the ringside at any Crufts show! Despite his historical link with fighting, his affectionate nature and love of family life and children are widely acknowledged.

The list of 26 breeds
in this group reads like a regional map
of Britain with the popular Border
Terrier a recent addition to the top 10 all
breeds list.

Originating from the border region
between England and Scotland, it is
described as essentially a working terrier
capable of going to ground after foxes.

The Bedlington, which bears a strong
resemblance to a lamb, is another
sporting north country dog.

From Ireland we have the Kerry Blue,
the Irish, the Glen of Imaal and the

Soft-coated Wheaten Terrier, a medium-sized dog with an unusually soft and silky coat.

Traditional 'English' and popular breeds must include the Bull Terrier, its miniature cousin and the Wire and Smooth Fox Terrier. 'King' of the Terriers is the majestic Airedale, standing up to 61cm (25 in) at the shoulder.

A later addition to the group in 1990 was the Parson Jack Russell, a breed based on the type favoured by the hunting Devon parson, the Reverend John Russell.

British-bred terriers are in great demand the world over, and recent years have seen a healthy growth in the import and export of stock to the advantage of many breeds.

POINTS TO REMEMBER

A well-known judge once told me to remember that all terriers believe they are twice their actual size.

Their popularity in the top 20 breeds cannot be denied, with West Highland Whites, Cairns and Staffords as popular as ever.

The indomitable terrier spirit endears them to family life as does their size, the majority of the 26 breeds in the group being short-legged. Regular brushing of any dog is essential and in terriers coat care must go one step further with 'stripping' (removal of surplus coat hair, fringes and feathering) if the correct texture and colour is to be maintained.

Terriers are sporting dogs with a tendency to chase and 'go to ground' if allowed. However, their larger than life personality and size make them a popular choice as a family pet.

Affectionately known as the 'King of Terriers' the Airedale was recognised as a pedigree breed in 1879. It was thought to be an amalgam of Harrier, Otterhound and Old English Terrier in its native Yorkshire. As with many terrier breeds, its coat requires careful attention.

Careful coat trimming has
maintained the correct outline of
this Airedale dog.

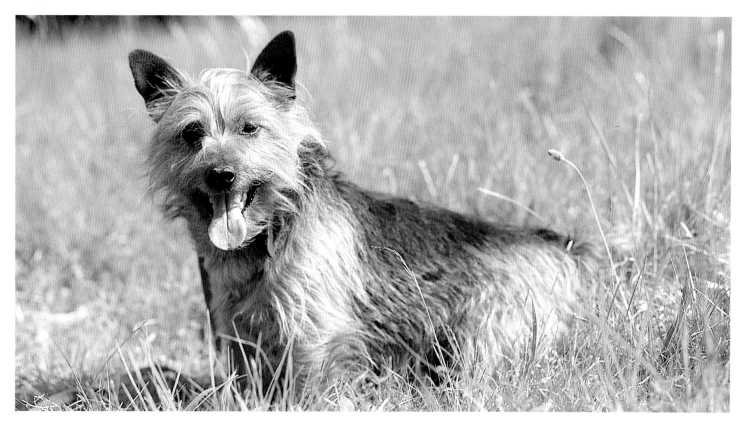

The Australian Terrier is a strong, rugged character and is essentially a working dog. He is a friendly extrovert with a harsh coat and alert expression. Note the harsh, dense, straight topcoat giving way to the underbody coat.

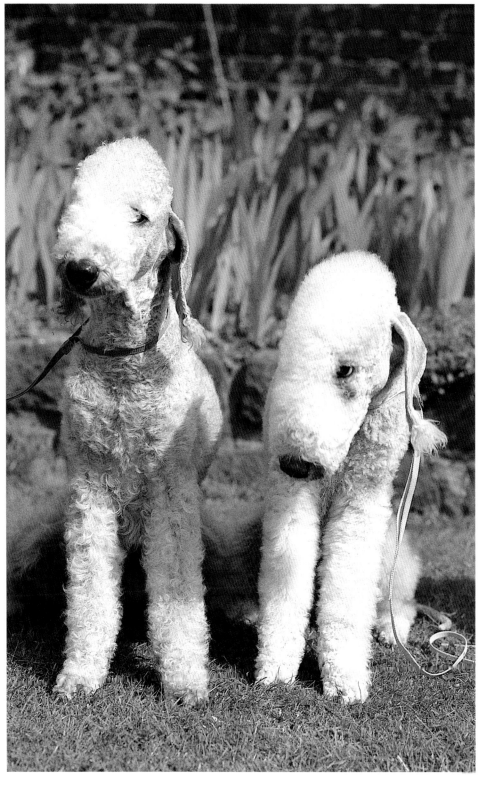

The Bedlington's lamb-like appearance belies a tough, graceful and muscular dog. He has a distinctive blue liver or sandy coloured coat and a light springy gait when walking.

Below: The Bull Terrier is a strongly built, four square Terrier. Traditionally all white in colour, they are also common in brindle, red, fawn and tri-colour.

Right: One of the most popular of Terriers, the Border is a natural looking worker, capable of doing a day's work in the field. It has a harsh, dense coat and close undercoat.

The Cairn is one of the most popular of the terrier breeds with its mischievous expression and harsh texture coat. A native of Scotland, it is described as strong, compact and workmanlike. Above is a grey brindle and, right and left, an attractive head study of a cream.

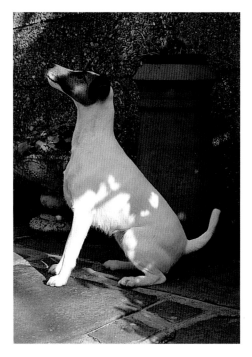

Above and right: The Smooth Fox Terrier is another of Britain's traditional breeds, which, along with the Wire Fox, was the most popular of terrier breeds over 100 years ago. As a hunting breed this breed has a lively, gay disposition.

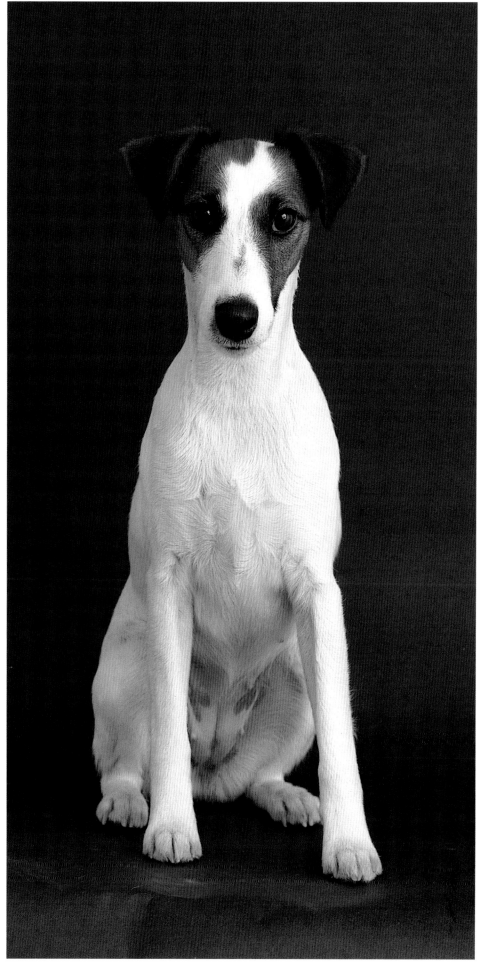

Left: The Dandie Dinmont is one of Scotland's traditional breeds. Note the distinctive head, silky hair on the domed skull and those wise, intelligent eyes.

The Wire Fox Terrier overtook its Smooth cousin in popularity until in Britain, in 1913, its own 'Wire' association catered for enthusiasts. As it is a 'coated' breed, due care and attention should be given to those furnishings so well illustrated here.

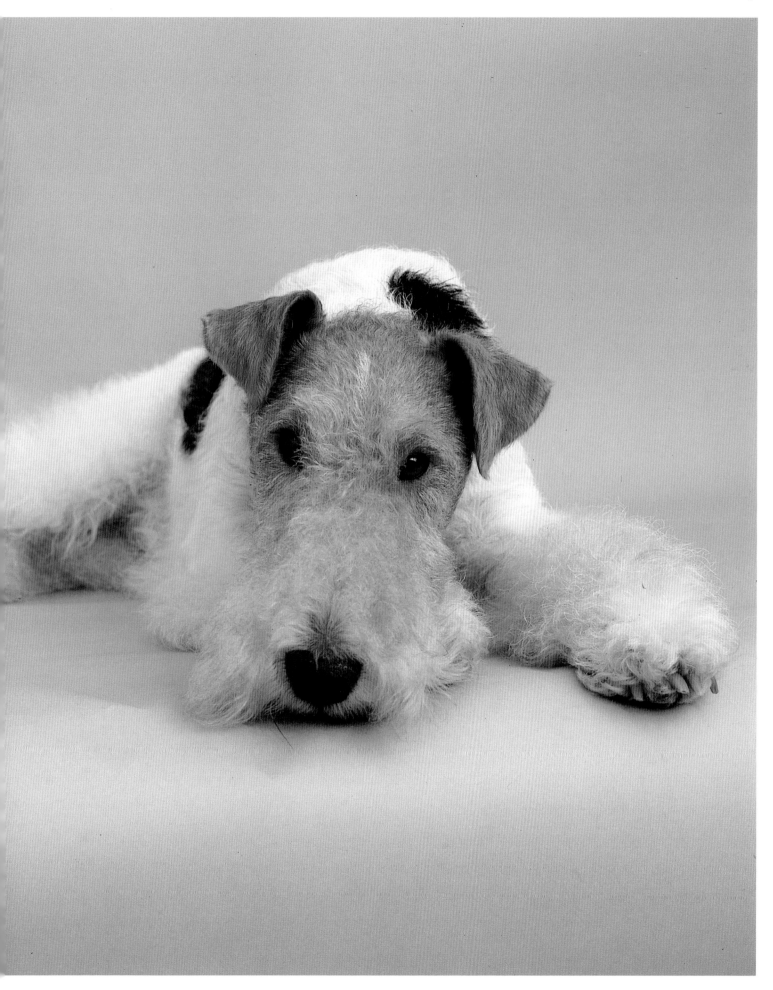

The Kerry Blue is noted for its steel blue coat and dark points. A compact, medium-sized terrier, it continues to attract good entries at principal shows.

Above: Derived from the Black and Tan Terrier of the 19th century, the Manchester is a keen, alert sporting companion. Its jet black coat is tipped with rich mahogany, noticable in this photograph on the muzzle and forelegs.

Right and opposite: The Norfolk and its close cousin, the Norwich, are typical short-legged Terriers. When trying to distinguish between the two breeds, the ears are the key - Norfolks **(illustrated here)** have ears which drop forward, whilst the Norwich sports alert-looking, erect ears.

The traditional Parson Jack Russell
Terrier gained Kennel Club
recognition in 1990. Developed by
the Reverend John Russell, the
breed type now closely resembles
the type much favoured by the
famous hunting West Country
parson.

The Scottish Terrier is a firm favourite amongst the traditional Scottish breeds. Bold but not aggressive, it is a loyal and faithful friend. Don't be deceived by those chocolate-box looks.

Left: The Staffordshire Bull Terrier is a smooth coated, agile dog for its medium to small size. It is noted for its intelligence and affectionate nature, particularly towards children.

Below and overleaf: The Welsh Terrier is a smart, compact breed, sometimes described as an Airedale in miniature, whereas its nearest cousin is the Lakeland. The breed was in the limelight in 1994 when a top winning specimen was best in show at Crufts.

Right and overleaf: Without doubt the most popular of Terriers, the West Highland White has remained a firm favourite, with two excellent examples of the breed going on to win best in show at Crufts in recent years.

UTILITY GROUP

UTILITY GROUP

For its size the Utility group has
considerable 'Best in show'
success at championship level.

It boasts the flamboyant and
immaculately presented Poodle in its
three varieties; the most popular breeds
in the group are the Shih Tzu, an ancient
breed of Tibetan origin, its close cousin
the Lhasa Apso, a breed greatly improved
by imported stock from the USA and the
ever popular Dalmatian with its
distinctive liver or black spots.

The traditional British breed, the
Bulldog, is now overshadowed by the
overseas additions to the group.

From the far east the popular Japanese Akita now accounts for a reasonable number of registrations, along with its compatriots the Japanese Shiba Inu and Japanese spitz. The Akita is the powerful, majestic national dog of Japan, the Shiba, another sturdy spitz, is a smaller dog, the popularity of which has escalated in the last 10 years.

Also from the orient is the familiar Chow Chow, a breed which features in Chinese art dating back over 2,000 years. More recently the popular Shar Pei has come to the fore during the last 20 years. Here, once again, both breeds share the same ancestors.

The Utility group also includes additional breeds from the continent in the shape of the German spitz (Klein and Mittel), adding greater weight to the possibility of a separate Spitz group in years to come.

At present the spitz types of breeds are distributed amongst the Toy, Utility, Working and Hound groups and there is a strong case for combining these to form one single group.

Twenty years ago there were only 15 breeds in the Utility group, whereas it now embraces 24 very diverse breeds.

POINTS TO REMEMBER

This group contains a wide variety of different breeds. The largest is the Standard Poodle and amongst the smallest its Toy 'cousin', the German Spitz (Klein) and the popular Shih Tzu.

Many of these are breeds with a profuse coat in the correct show trim, but which demand considerable care and attention if they are to remain attractive. The spitz breeds in particular share a distinctive thick 'stand off' coat which is part of their charm.

The group also includes the Bulldog, a firm favourite, the Dalmatian and French Bulldogs - all smooth coated breeds. Close care and attention must be given to selection when considering ownership of the widely diverse characters in this group.

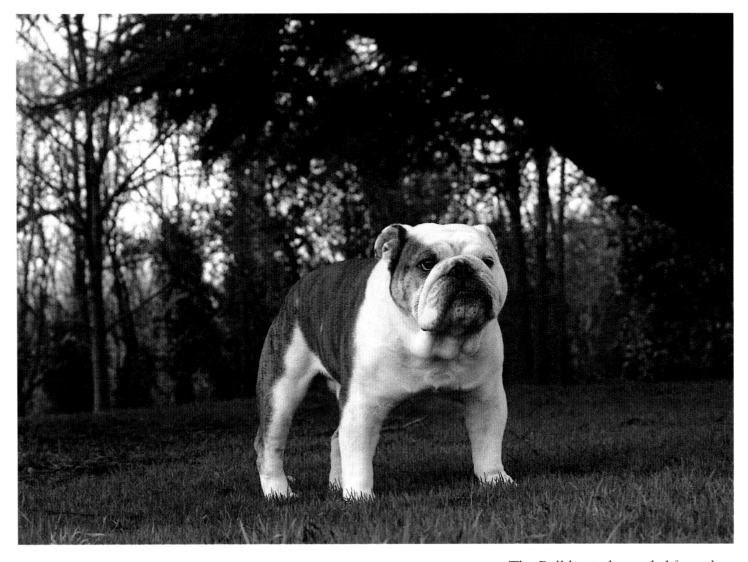

The Bulldog is descended from the 19th century bull-baiting dogs. Now a thickset, four-square breed its appearance has been carefully maintained. It is single minded to the point of obstinacy, so enthusiasts have to be committed!

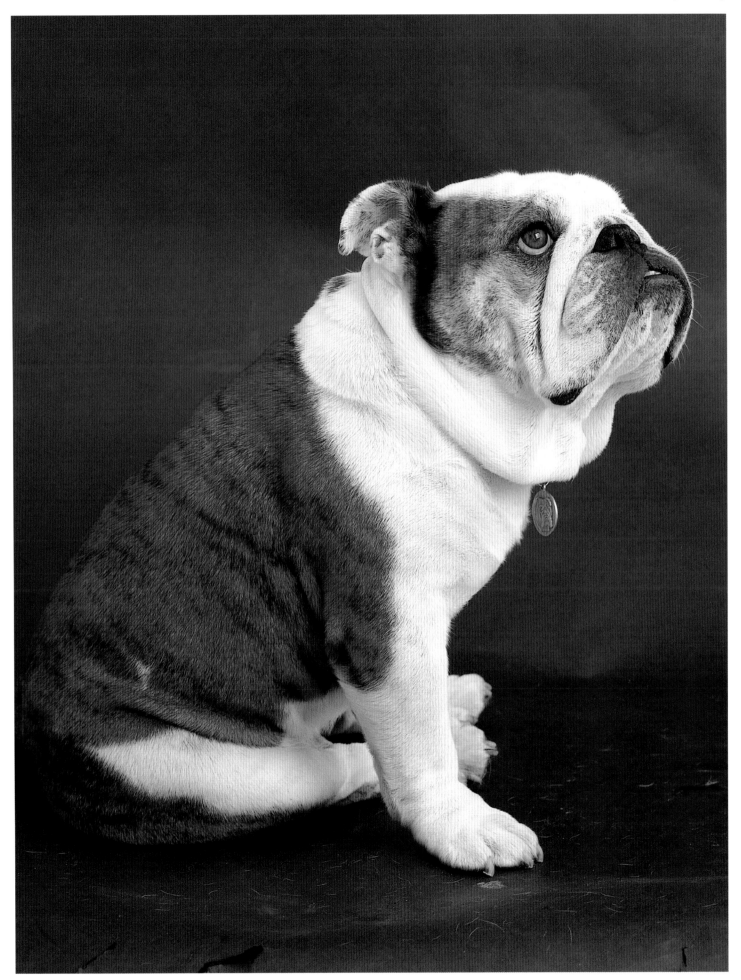

Dogs

Chow Chows originate from the orient, where they were used as a guard dog. They are a broad-chested, muscular dog with an unusual blue tongue. Note the thick coat on this comparatively young dog pictured **below right**.

Left: The Dalmatian, a native of central Europe, was bred and kept as a 'carriage' dog in the 18th century to protect those on long journeys from attack by wolves. Its distinctive spotting in black or liver should be evenly distributed on a white coat.

Below: The Japanese Spitz is a small spitz type which has become popular in recent years. The 'stand-off' pure white coat gives way to a thick undercoat, both of which need care and attention.

Dogs

The Keeshond is another spitz type with a profuse, harsh coat and dense ruff shown to advantage here. The tail carriage should be close and held over the body **(overleaf)**.

Right: The Lhasa Apso was introduced to Britain in 1928 and it is one of several Tibetan breeds. Popular and successful bloodlines now exist in Britain, America and Scandinavia.

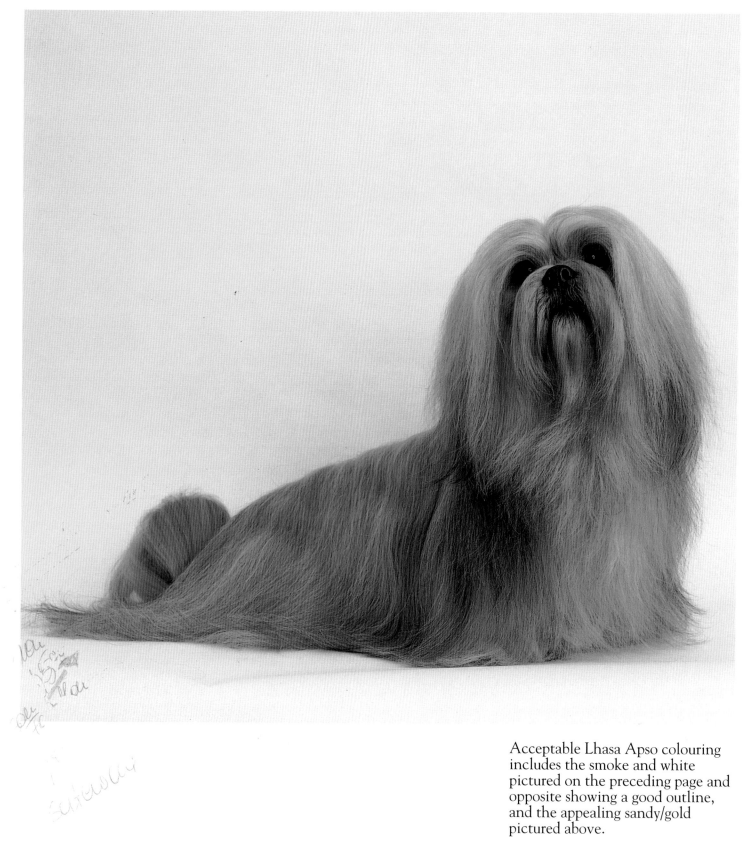

Acceptable Lhasa Apso colouring includes the smoke and white pictured on the preceding page and opposite showing a good outline, and the appealing sandy/gold pictured above.

The Poodle in its Standard form was originally a gundog worked extensively in western Europe but originating from France. Sporting dogs had a full coat but would have their hindquarters clipped to enable them to swim in pursuit of game. Such clipping is thought to have given rise to the fashionable way in which the ladies of the Montmartre presented the Miniature and Toy Poodles which descended from the Standard.

Below: The Schnauzer family originates from Germany. These dogs were bred mainly as 'yard' dogs and to cut down vermin. The Miniature illustrated here shows off the breed's hard textured and wiry coat.

Right: The Schipperke, or Barge Dog, is just that - a small breed developed to act as a guard on the canal boats on Flemish canals. His name in Flemish means "little captain" which refers as much to his self-importance as to his nautical air!

Maintaining the far eastern theme, the Shih Tzu harks from China and is often confused with the Lhasa. The coat is long and dense and on this page we see a gold and white and a black and white, groomed in a more natural style.

Above: This gold and white Shih Tzu shows off the heavily plumed tail correctly carried over the back.

Right and overleaf: The Tibetan Spaniel is a native of the roof of the world, where it is a dog with great status due to its religious significance. Kept in monasteries and temples, it is often the only animal allowed in such holy places. It has enjoyed increased popularity in the UK over the last 50 years.

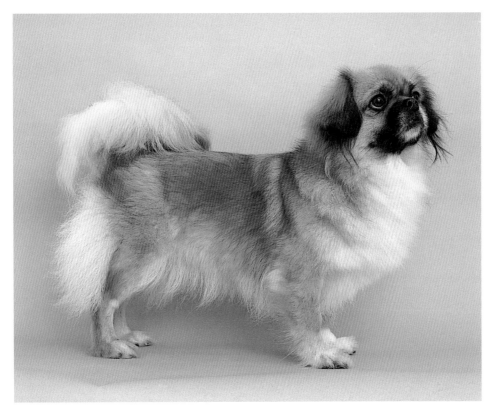

Right and overleaf: The Tibetan Terrier, which is not classified as a terrier breed, is another product of close breeding in the monasteries of Tibet, to produce a singular type. Sometimes compared to the Old English Sheepdog in miniature, the breed has a profuse, wavy or straight top coat and all colours except chocolate or liver are permissable.

WORKING GROUP

WORKING GROUP

The 50 breeds in the Working group
include all the pastoral and flock
guarding breeds.

Breeds native to the British Isles include
the Collie type in all its varieties.
Scotland is justified in its claim that it
developed these breeds, although a fairly
recent addition to the group, and the
show ring, was the Border Collie. This
highly intelligent breed is still actively
worked in obedience and agility alike.

Other native types include the popular
Old English Sheepdog, the more obscure
but recently revived Lancashire Heeler
and the Welsh Corgi in the Pembroke and
Cardigan varieties.

This breed was inter-bred until the early 1930s, when separate classification was scheduled at shows.

The German Shepherd continues to attract its enthusiasts and maintains pole position in the popularity stakes.

Second place goes to the Boxer, with an almost equal third slot going to the Rough Collie and the Shetland Sheepdog.

A whole range of draught dogs from the lowlands and central Europe now dominates a group which was created in 1963 when the non-sporting breeds were

split to form the Utility and
Working groups.

Add to these the striking Australian
Cattle Dog from down under, the Swedish
Lapphund and Vallhund, the almost
Poodle-like Portuguese Water Dog, the
famous and much loved St. Bernard and
the Mastiff and mollosoid types from Italy
and Tibet, and it is easy to see what a
cosmopolitan group this is!

Once again here is a group under close
scrutiny and ripe for partition into
pastoral or shepherding breeds sections.

POINTS TO REMEMBER

Over 50 breeds make up the
'Working' element and here we have
the largest group with the
largest dogs.

Space, time and exercise are
essentials when considering
ownership of any breed in this
group. There are few short-legged
examples and most have the profuse
coat typical of pastoral and flock
guarding breeds from
hostile climates.

Some of the shepherding breeds
have a thick double coat which
requires special care and attention,
particularly after exercising in
wet weather.

Along with size this group can lay
claim to brains as well, for many of
its breeds also acquit themselves
well in obedience, working trials
and agility.

The Alaskan Malamute is regarded as the national breed of Alaska. Immensely powerful, it is a natural sled dog and faithful companion.

The Australian Cattle Dog is the product of imported stock and carries the bloodlines of several working breeds. Note the inquisitive, intelligent expression, large fox-like ears, and 'brush' of a tail.

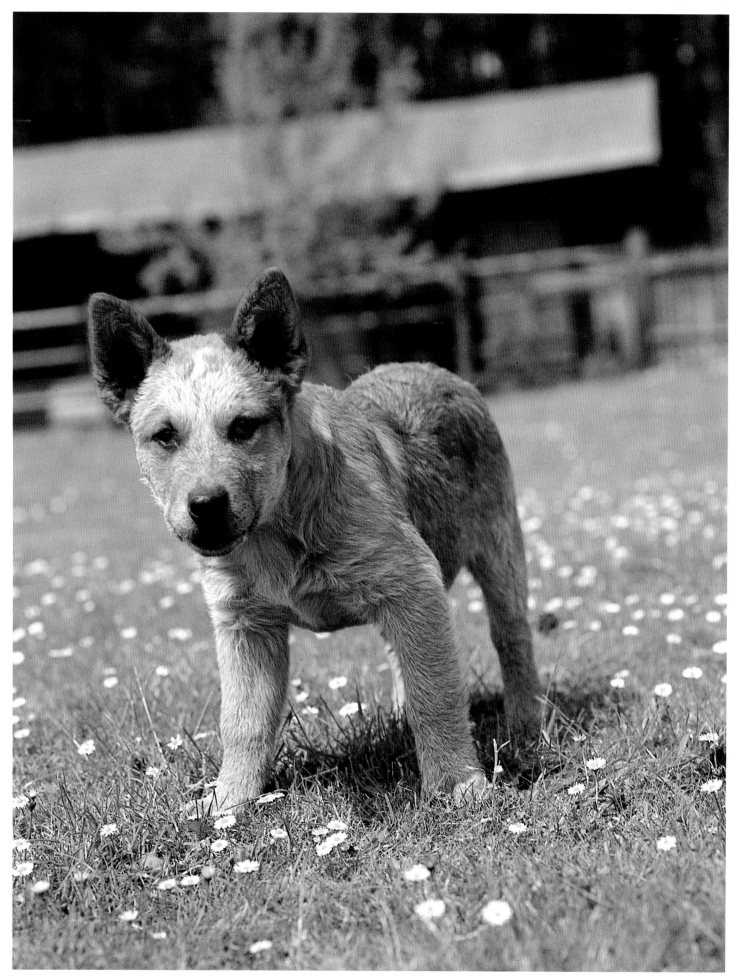

The Bearded Collie was only recognised as an individual breed 50 years ago but its roots go back over a century to Scotland and the collie-types bred for their intelligence and herding abilities. Alert, lively and self-confident, its slate grey, reddish fawn or brown coat demands close attention.

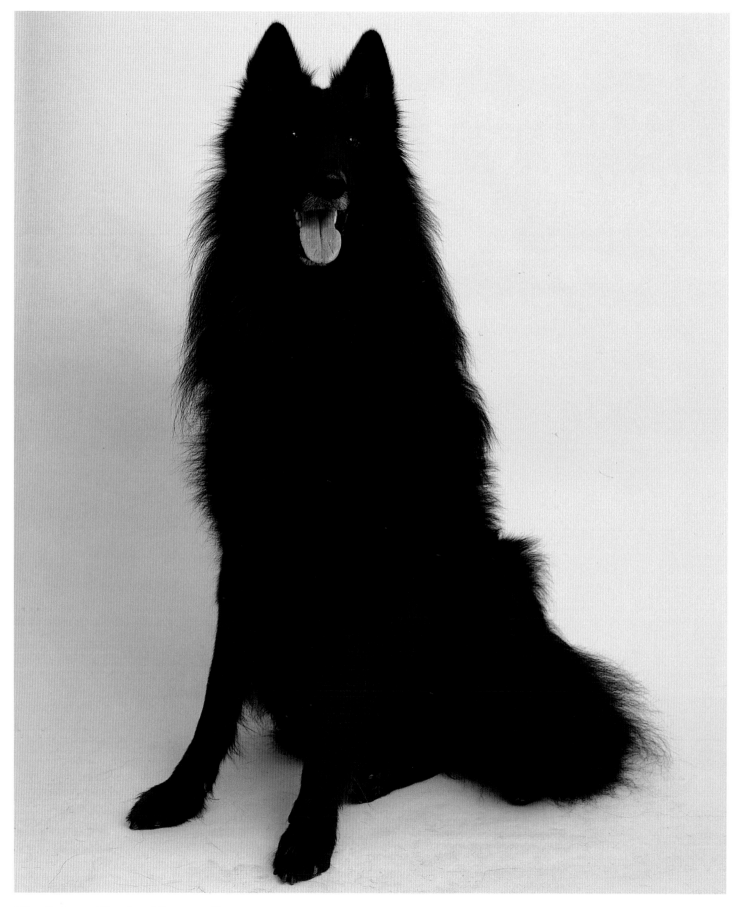

The Belgian Shepherd Dog in all its four varieties is a herding dog of lowland Europe. The three main varieties vary in coat colour with the Laekenois (right) having a distinctive harsh, wiry, reddish fawn coat. The Kennel Club has now decided to recognise all four varieties as one breed.

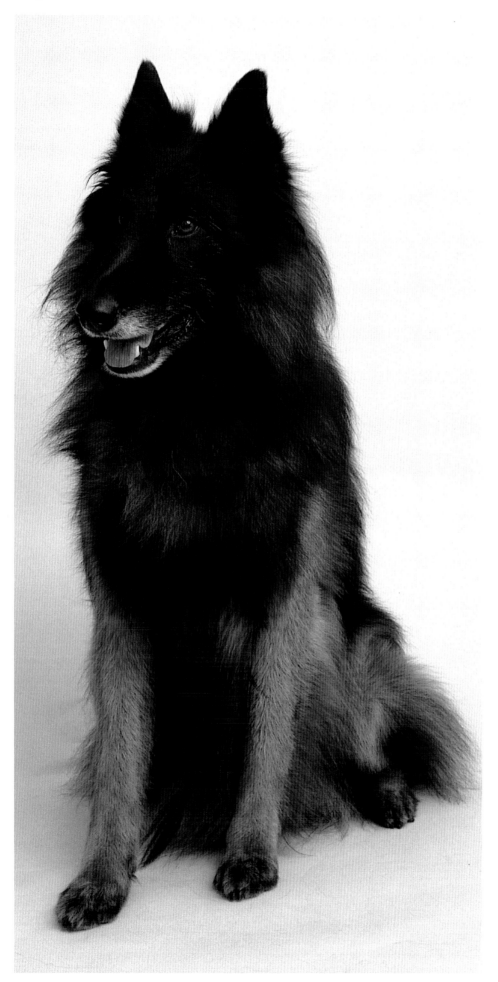

Within the Belgian Shepherd fraternity enthusiasts still advocate the individual varieties such as the all black Groenendael **(page 166)**, the Tervueren **(left)** and the black masked Malinois **(right)**.

Left: Described as every child's idea of what a dog should look like, the Bernese Mountain Dog hails from the Bernese Oberland region of Switzerland. Used as a draught dog on hill farms, it has an impeccably good nature and friendly character.

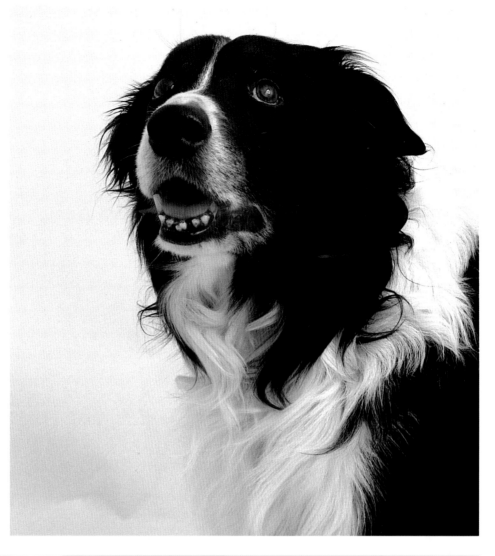

Right and below: Recognised as the world's finest sheepdog, the Border Collie has its origins in the hills of Scotland. The considerable success achieved by the breed at Obedience and Working Trial level resulted in growing interest in the breed as a show dog, and in Kennel Club registration in the 1980s.

Above: The Bouvier des Flandres is a powerfully built drover's dog from the low countries which was used extensively as a messenger or ambulance dog in the First World War. His tough, wiry outcoat has a fine, soft undercoat.

Below and overleaf: The popular
Boxer is another Germanic breed,
the name of which is derived from
the way it punches the air in play.
Devotees appreciate its biddable,
fearless temperament and here we
see good examples of the
brindle/white and red/white
colouring.
In the USA, the American Kennel
Club requires Boxers being shown
to have their ears docked.

Dogs

Right and overleaf: The Briard is an ancient 'Berger' sheepdog from the continent which, despite achieving some popularity in the UK 100 years ago, has only increased in numbers in the last 15 years. Here we see some fine examples of the black and fawn shading in its profuse coat.

Below and overleaf: The Bullmastiff is a popular and slightly smaller version of the traditional Mastiff from which it was derived. It was used as a guard by gamekeepers to protect their masters' estates from poachers.

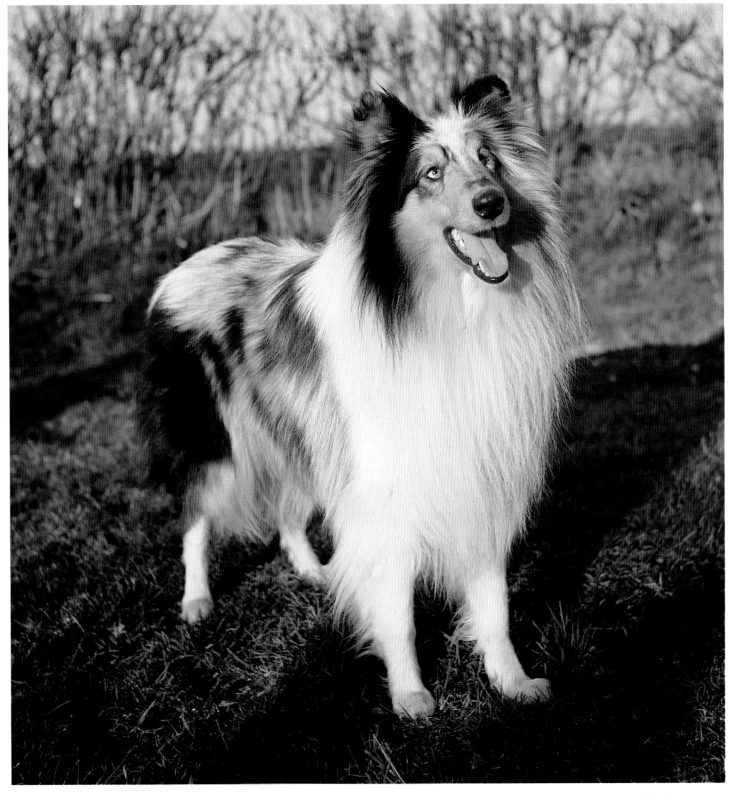

Above: As one of Scotland's traditional herding breeds the Rough Collie was admired by Queen Victoria in the 1860s on one of her first visits to the Balmoral estates. Her love of the breed assured its future popularity. This blue merle has the permitted blue or blue flecked eyes.

The origins of the Dobermann Pinscher can be traced back to the 1860s and a German tax collector, Herr Louis Dobermann, who wanted a dog for protection on his rounds. Thought to have been crossed with a pinscher or terrier type, the Dobermann is a stylish, loyal companion which needs firm handling.

Above: The Eskimo Dog is a powerfully built, heavy coated breed and, as the name implies, the haulage dog of the Eskimo tribe. It has terrific stamina and a thick double coat to enable it to survive the worst Arctic conditions.

Right: The Estrela Mountain Dog from Portugal is typical of many European herding and guarding breeds. Note the deep chest and broad, massive head of this powerful breed.

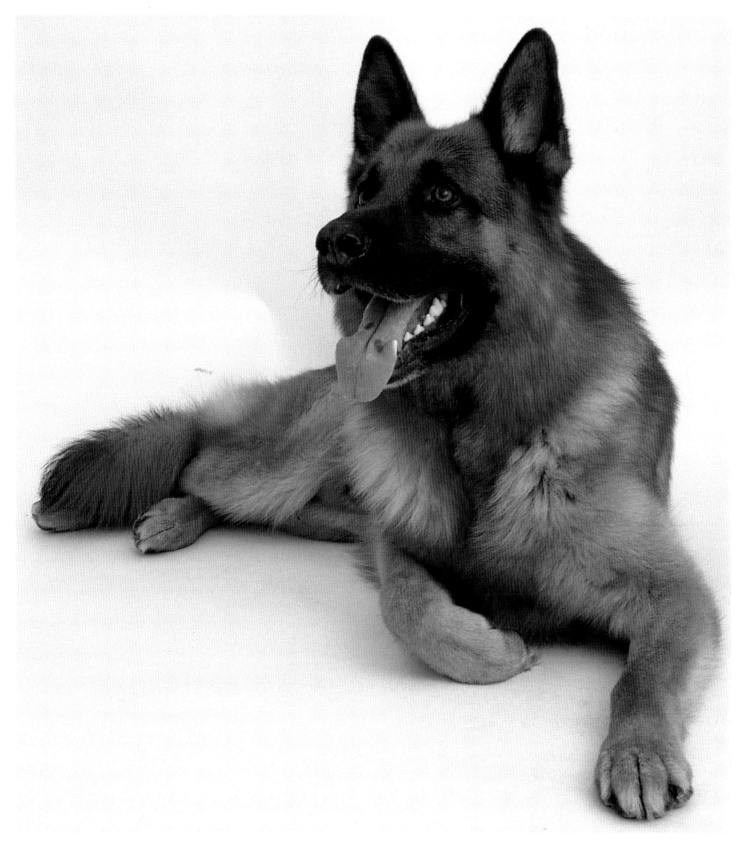

The German Shepherd Dog was the most popular dog in Britain in 1926 when it was known as the Alsatian Wolf Dog. Its qualities were appreciated by soldiers in the First World War in which it was used as an ambulance and messenger dog in front lines.

Undoubtedly the most popular breed worldwide, with distinguished service in the police and the armed services, it has a loyal following of enthusiasts. Known as the Alsatian until the early 1970s, German Shepherd bloodlines have definite English and German types. Recent years have seen increased interest in the importation of continental stock which has made its mark in the showring today. Note the alert expression of this versatile working dog.

The popular Great Dane is of German origin and was used in the 17th century as a coursing and hunting dog. The breed today is much finer in bone and body but an adult male can weigh in at 54 kg (120 lbs). The popular fawn with black mask is shown here with the striking harlequin **(below and overleaf)**.

The Hungarian Puli has a unique corded coat shown off to advantage by this grey **(above)** and black masked apricot **(right)**. Originally a herder and drover in its native country, it was first exhibited in Britain around 1950 and has increased in popularity in the last 15 years.

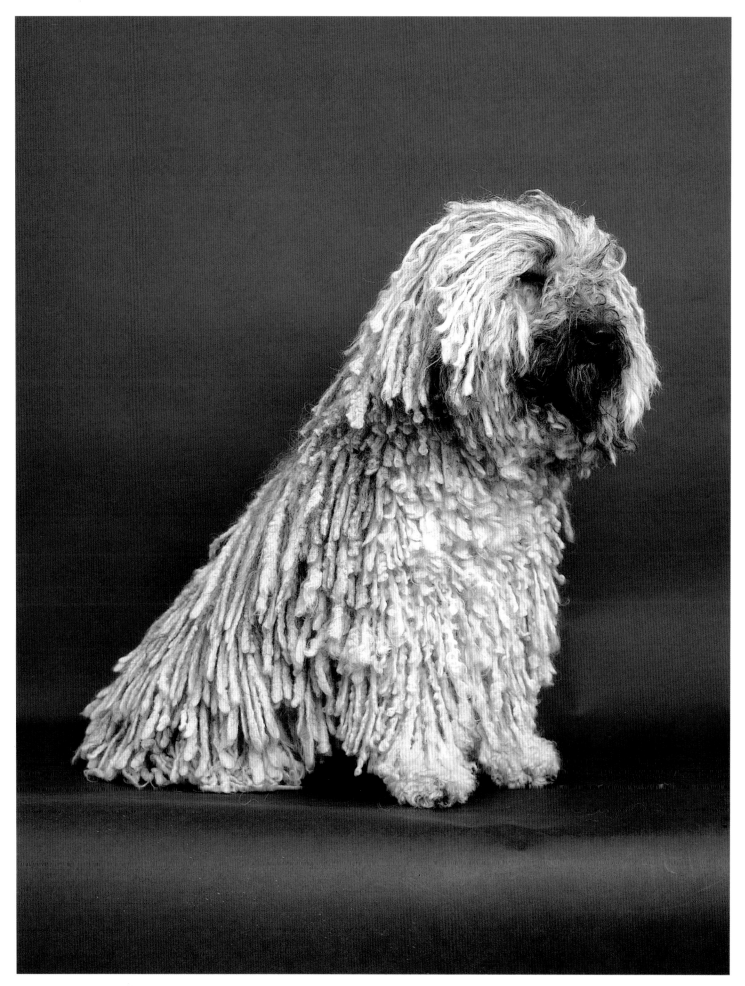

Dogs

The Newfoundland is another superb water dog which started life as a draught dog in its native Canada. This gentle giant has a natural eagerness to please and an adult male can weigh up to 69kgs (138 lbs). Note the huge paws on this puppy **(right)** and the attractive brown **(opposite)**.

Above: The Norwegian Buhund is a typical spitz breed, with ancient origins in the Icelandic Dog of over 1,000 years ago. Commonly seen in a wheaten jacket **(above)**, they are also acceptable in wolf sable and black coats.

Right and overleaf: The Old English Sheepdog or 'Bobtail' was developed as a working breed in the west country region in the 19th century. It is a profusely coated breed with a wide appeal, but time must be allocated to regular grooming.

Above: Often mistaken for a 'poodle cross' the Portuguese Water Dog is a traditional water breed clipped out over the hindquarters to facilitate swimming in its function of assisting local fishermen to retrieve nets. A keen guard dog, its profuse coat protects it from cold sea temperatures.

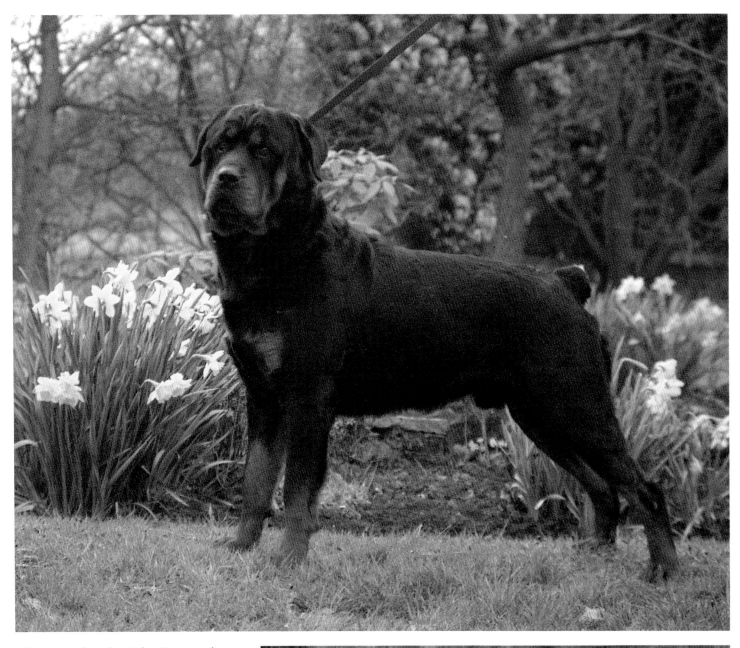

Above and right: The Rottweiler, essentially a guarding breed, originates from Rottweil in Germany. It is noted as a loyal working companion and several police forces have used it for patrol work.

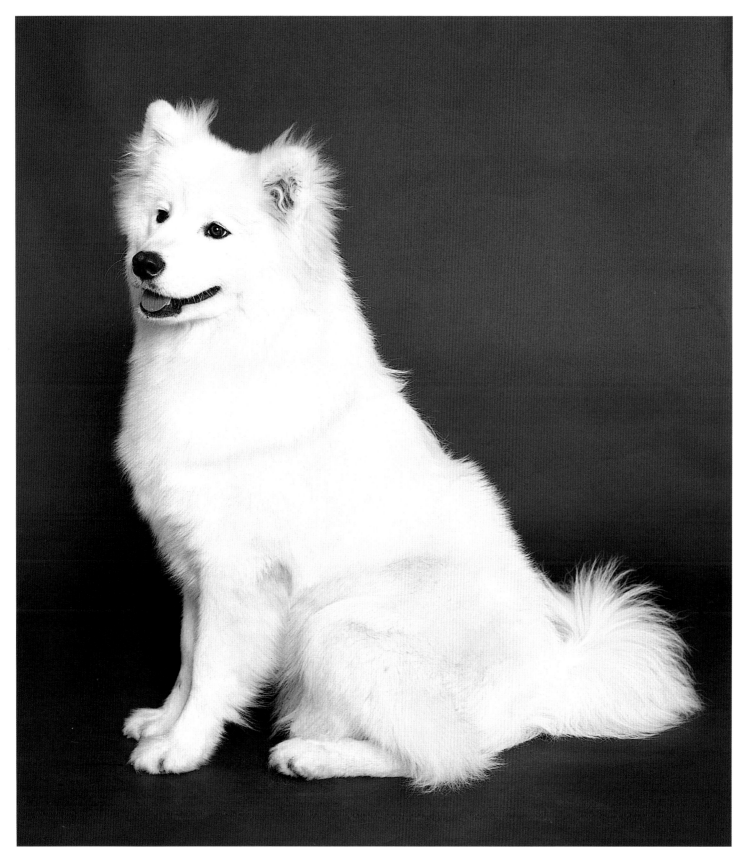

Left: The St Bernard was probably brought to Switzerland by the Roman army's northerly push into Europe. In the 1700s references to 'rescue dogs' working out of the Hospice founded by Archdeacon Bernard de Menthon suggest that the use of dogs was an established routine. It is generally accepted that those dogs were finer boned and had less substance than examples of the breed seen today.

Above: An attractive member of the spitz family, the Samoyed originates from Siberia, where it worked as a sled dog, and as a herding and guarding breed. The breed is noted for its melting 'smile', in evidence here!

Left and overleaf: The Shetland Sheepdog is a collie in miniature originally from that northern Scottish isle. A beautiful, intelligent and alert dog, it has a double thick coat, shown to advantage on this sable and white and tricolour.

The Shetland Sheepdogs' mane, frill and feathering are evident in these photos. Note the alert expression and ear carriage **(below)**.

The Siberian Husky originates from north east Asia where it was used as a sledge dog for the Chukshi, a nomadic tribe which inhabited the frozen steppes. The breed boasts a double thick medium length coat to enable it to work in extremely cold climates. The breed is still favoured by sledge enthusiasts today and teams of Huskies regularly compete in timed trials on forest tracks during the winter season.

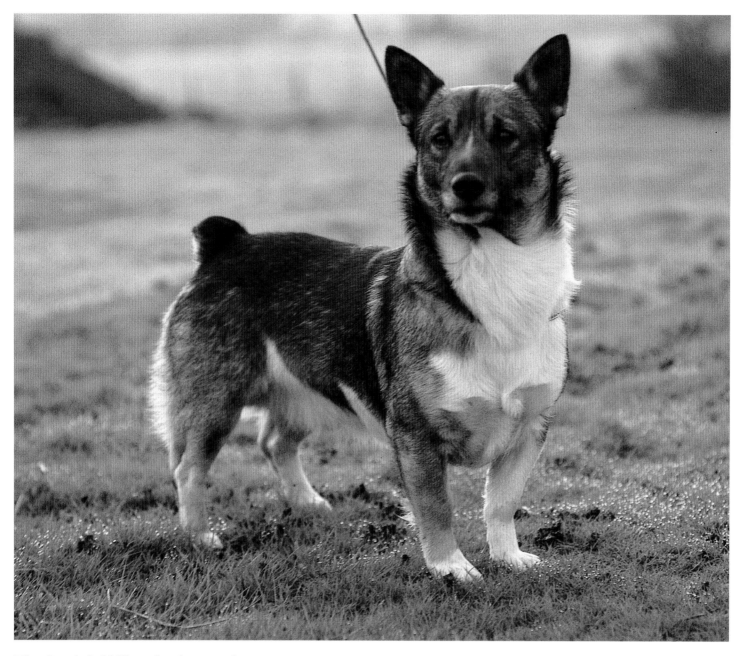

The Swedish Vallhund only gained
formal recognition in the 1940s,
and here again is a typical spitz
type with cattle herding qualities
similar to the Welsh Corgi which
must be a distant relative.

The tailed Cardigan Welsh Corgi **(above)** and its close Pembroke cousin **(below and right)** were not recognised as separate breeds until 1934. Essentially a cattle droving breed, they have an appealing foxy expression. The British Royal family also popularised the breed with fine specimens often appearing in family photographs.

TOY GROUP

TOY GROUP

As well as their preoccupation with the developments taking place throughout the British Empire, the Victorians also took a keen interest in zoology and stock-keeping, with a particular focus on the Toy Dog group of breeds.

During the Victorian era sporting dog exhibitions and shows extended their classification to reflect
"...the increased popularity of these smaller, cosseted dogs particularly favoured by the ladies."

So said Mr Cruft in 1890 when Cruft's own show incorporated Toy Dog Club classes to enhance the show's authority.

Pomeranians were a popular spitz breed
in miniature, the Pekingese were greatly
favoured by Queen Victoria and Pugs,
too, were widespread at that time.

Recent years have seen a sustained
increase in Cavalier King Charles
Spaniel registrations, whilst the
Yorkshire Terrier remains the most
popular of the Toy breeds.

Once again the overseas influence on
breeds listed within this group is
obvious. In a comparatively short period
the Bichon Frisé, an appealing white dog
of French origin, has attracted wide
interest and several breed clubs have
emerged to serve these enthusiasts.

The oriental connection via the Pekingese is obvious, but less well known is the Japanese Chin, formerly the Japanese Spaniel.

The Chinese Crested, apart from its crest of hair and tufts on the feet, is a unique hairless dog.

The demands of modern living prevent many people from owning a large dog. Those who don't favour the sporting breeds often turn to this group for a companion or a family pet more suited to their town life.

Nevertheless, the 22 members of the Toy group are truly '*multum in parvo*'.

POINTS TO REMEMBER

This is the smallest group with the
smallest dogs, but what variety
lies within it!

It is easy to say that these breeds
'lend themselves to modern living,'
but close attention has to be paid to
these Toys if they are to become
part of your life.

Coats range from smooth to
profuse, and in terms of character,
these dogs range from the aloof to
the gay Cavalier which has to be
everyone's friend.

A study has indicated that these
breeds are more favoured by the
elderly and retired, but such
statistics are confounded by the
emergence of the Yorkshire Terrier
and the Cavalier King Charles
Spaniel in the top 10 of all breeds
over many years.

Remember, despite their smaller
appetites and in some cases the need
for less exercise, they need every bit
as much care and attention as their
larger cousins.

Dogs

The impish Affenpinscher and the Miniature Pinscher were the same breed until in 1896 it was decided to separate the different coated varieties. A game, alert little dog, it is the smallest of all the Pinscher family. The dog on the left with 'prick' ears is a typical German import.

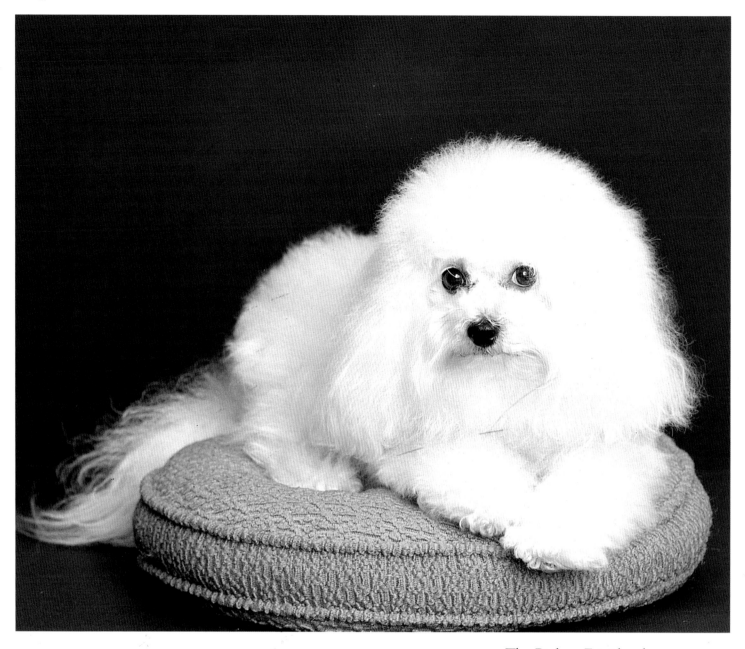

The Bichon Frisé has become a popular breed in recent years but its French origins go back to the 14th century, when Italian merchants were said to have brought these attractive white dogs from the Canary Islands to mainland Europe. The breed was favoured by the royal courts of Europe. and consequently was portrayed in many oil paintings of the time.

The Cavalier King Charles Spaniel is the second most popular of all Toy breeds and its forerunner was the toy spaniel in favour at the time of King Charles II. The variety of colours shown here ranges through the solid ruby (or rich fawn), the blenheim (chestnut and white), black and tan and tricolour. Described as an active, graceful but sparkling character, it is easy to see why it appeals as a family dog.

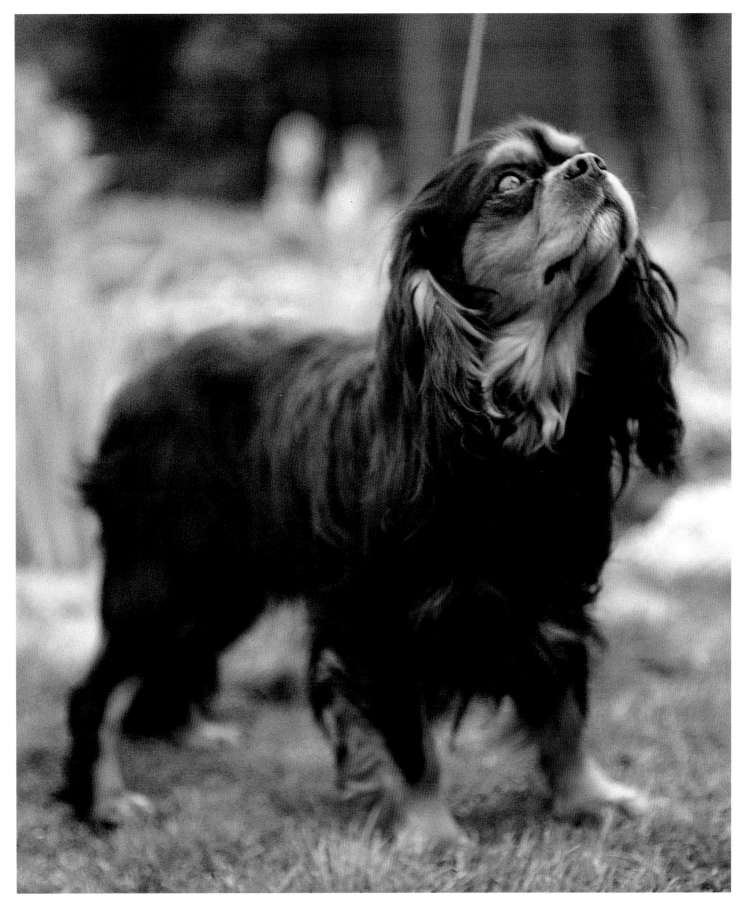

Above: The black and tan
Cavalier has raven black with tan
markings above the eyes and on
the cheeks, chest and legs.

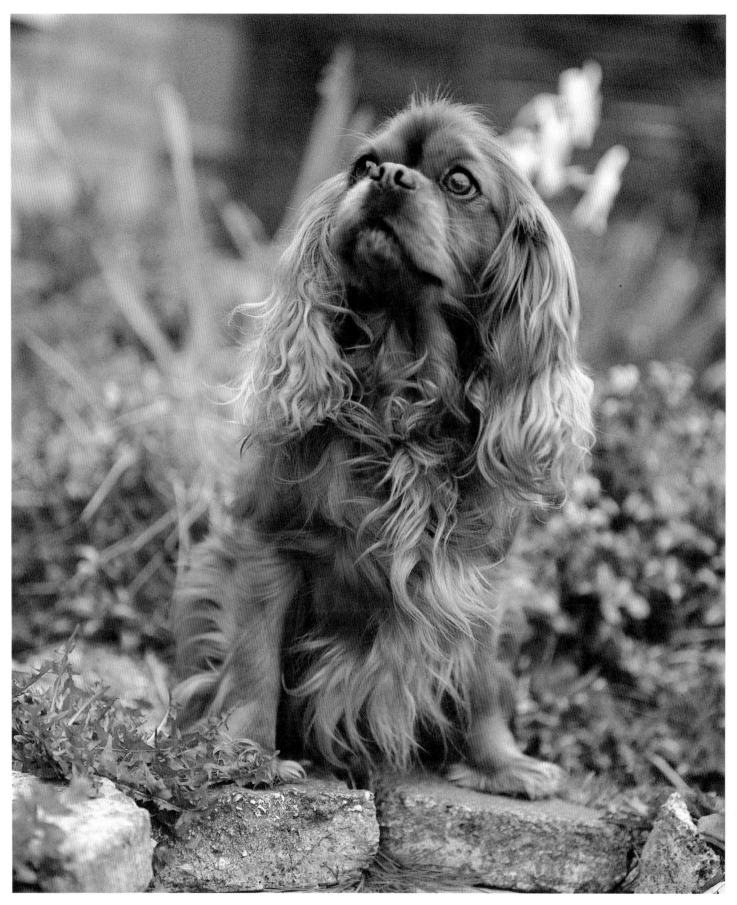

Above: The whole coloured rich
red ruby Cavalier has no
white markings.

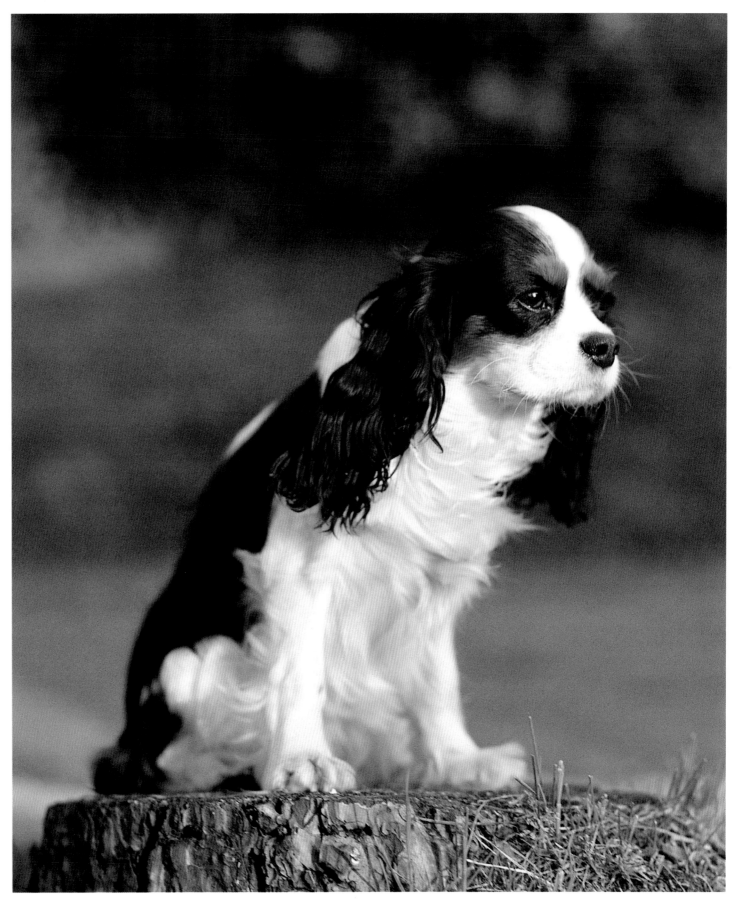

Above: The tri-colour Cavalier has
a well broken black and white coat
with tan markings.

Above: The classic popular blenheim Cavalier showing the rich chestnut markings on a predominantly white coat.

The Longcoat Chihuahua **(right)** pictured here and its close cousin the Smoothcoat **(left)** are the world's smallest breeds of dog. The first Chihuahua was registered by the American Kennel Club in 1904. Whilst it is generally accepted that they emanate from the Mexican state after which they were named, they were thought to have arrived there from Pacific trade routes to the far east. Despite their size they have a bold temperament.

Note the classic 'apple dome' head
and large round eyes set well apart
on this attractive cream
Smoothcoat Chihuahua.

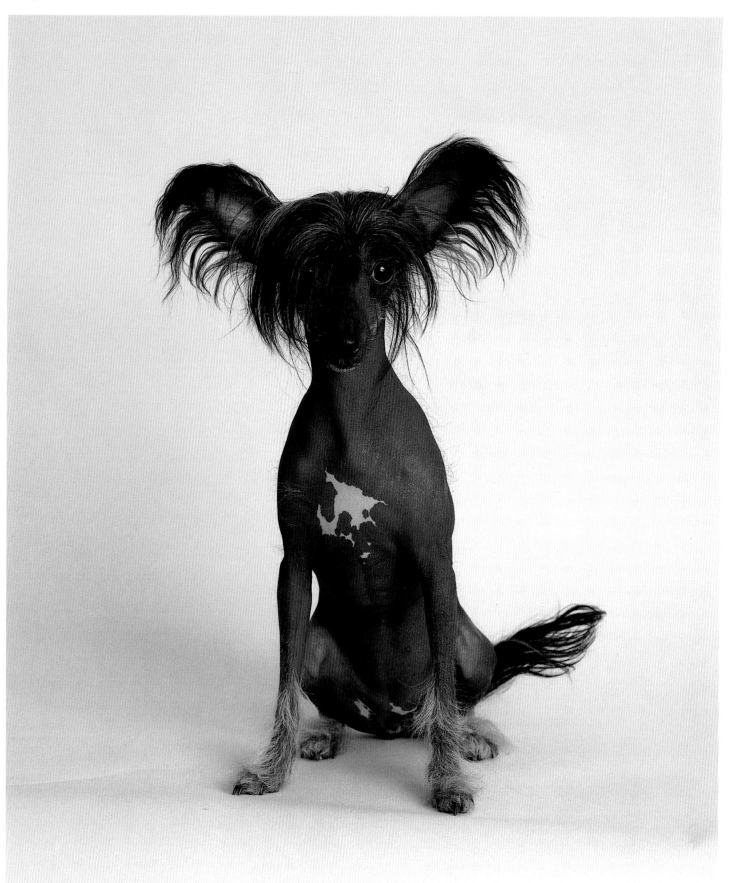

Whilst the origins of the Chinese Crested Dog are obvious, examples of other hairless dogs exist in Africa, Turkey and Mexico.

The featherings on the feet, tail and ears are particularly distinctive. The body skin can be any solid colour or mottled.

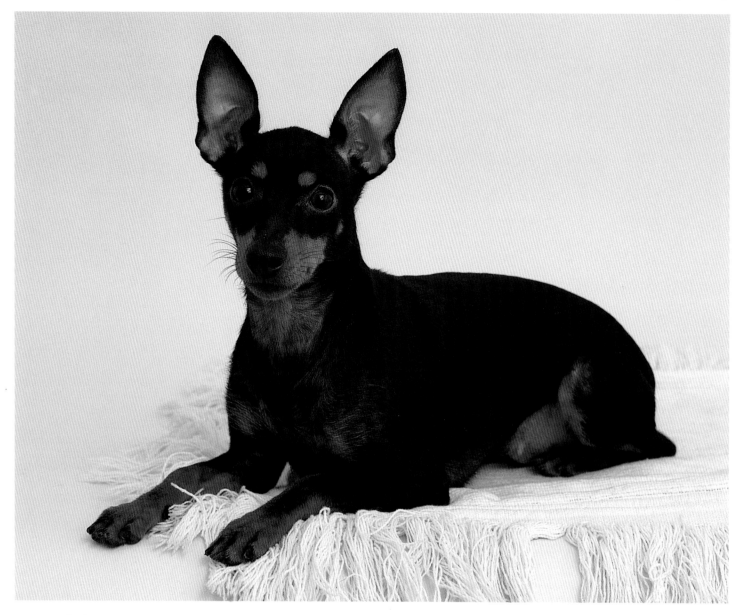

Originally known as the Toy Black
and Tan Terrier, the English Toy
Terrier is essentially a Manchester
Terrier in miniature. It gained its
reputation in the ratpits of 19th
century Britain where its catching
technique was tested in
competition with other dogs.

The Griffon Bruxellois showing the smooth and rough coated varieties. A native of Belgium, it is an intelligent, well-balanced little dog with an impish, monkey-like expression.

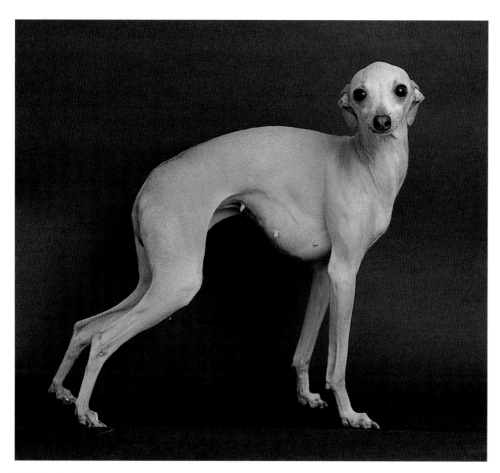

Opposite and left: The Italian Greyhound is a slender and elegant greyhound in miniature. Despite its delicate appearance, it is a fearless character with a gentle, loving nature.

Below and overleaf: The Löwchen is often known as the Little Lion Dog because of the traditional lion clip in which it is presented in the show ring. Its origins are European, probably as a member of the Bichon family, and it has gained popularity over the last 20 years.

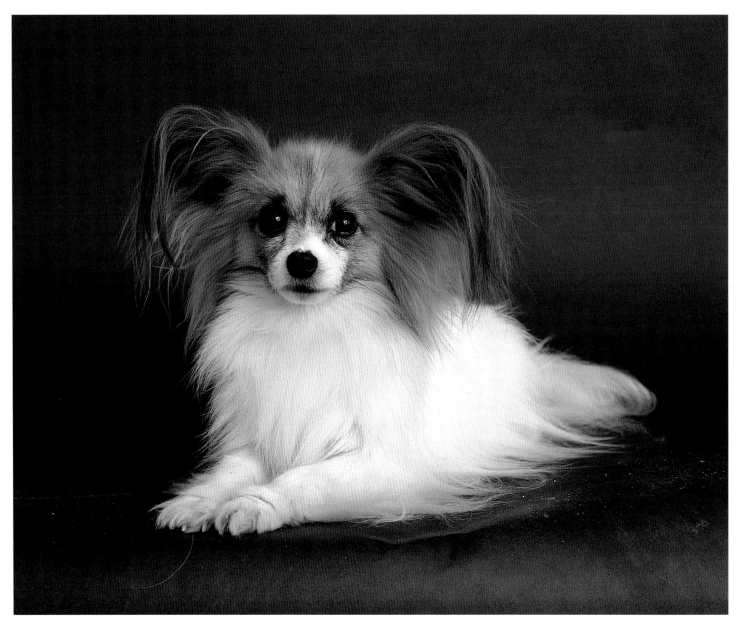

The Papillon originated in central
Europe evolving as the Dwarf
Spaniel in the 16th century. Note
the profuse ear fringes and alert
expression on these examples of
the breed.

The Pekingese was the sacred dog of China, and its history is carefully recorded in carvings, bronzes and paintings going back to the 8th century. The dogs were introduced to Britain in 1860 after the sacking of the Summer Palace in Peking during the Boxer Rebellion. A fawn and white Pekingese is said to have been passed on to Queen Victoria at the time. The fawn with a black mask is the most popular colour but here we also see an appealing black.

Above and preceding page: A black masked fawn Pekingese. Note the broad skull and required profuse coat.

Right and overleaf: As a dainty toy spitz breed, the Pomeranian was a great favourite of Queen Victoria. Its attractive, straight, harsh coat is evident in these orange **(overleaf)** and pale orange **(right)** examples.

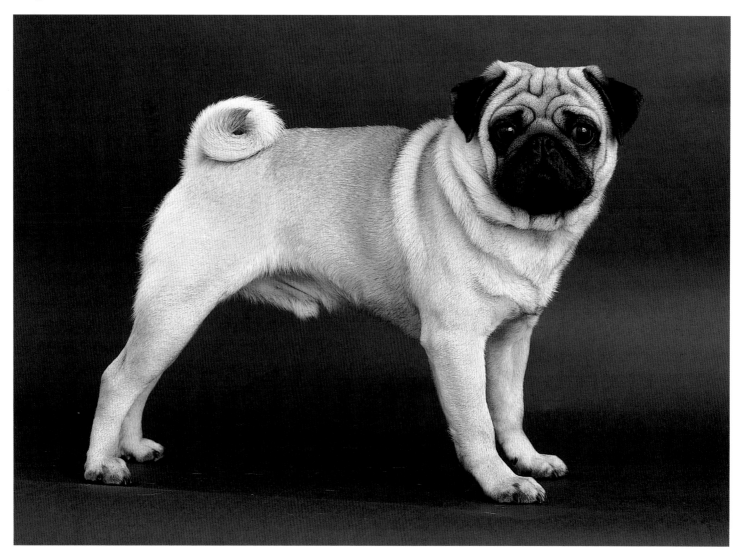

The Pug is a native of China and was said to have been brought into Europe by Dutch traders. Clearly defined wrinkles are an important part of the head and expression in this dignified, intelligent dog.

The Yorkshire Terrier is the most popular of all the Toy breeds and overall is rarely out of the top three. A glamorous and fashionable pet in the late 19th century, it attracted large entries at shows, but its origins were modest by comparison. Now considerably miniaturised its predecessors were longer in the leg to enable them to catch vermin. The Yorkshire was thought to have been an amalgam of various sporting Terriers to produce this dog with an attractive silky steel blue coat and tan head markings. Although placed in the Toy group its terrier instinct remains as strong as ever.

I N D E X

Dogs